The
HERITAGE BOOK
2000

The

HERITAGE
BOOK

2000

Edna McCann

HarperCollins*Publishers*Ltd

THE HERITAGE BOOK 2000
Copyright © 1999 by Edna McCann.
All rights reserved. No part of this book may be used or reproduced in any manner
whatsoever without prior written permission except in the case of brief quotations
embodied in reviews. For information address HarperCollins Publishers Ltd,
55 Avenue Road, Suite 2900, Toronto, Ontario, Canada M5R 3L2.

http://www.harpercanada.com

HarperCollins books may be purchased for educational, business, or sales promotional
use. For information please write: Special Markets Department, HarperCollins
Canada, 55 Avenue Road, Suite 2900, Toronto, Ontario, Canada M5R 3L2.

Acknowledgements:

Page 11. "Skaters at Dusk" from *The Crystal Fountain* by Grace Noll Crowell
is reprinted courtesy of HarperCollins.

Page 48. Excerpt from *A Touch of Wonder* by Arthur Gordon
is reprinted courtesy of Fleming H. Revell Publishers

Page 81. From *Space* by James Michener. Copyright © 1982 by James Michener.
Reprinted by permission of Random House, Inc.

Pages 97–98. From *Gift from the Sea* by Anne Morrow Lindbergh.
Copyright © 1955, 1975, renewed 1983 by Anne Morrow Lindbergh.
Reprinted by permission of Pantheon Books, a division of Random House, Inc.

First HarperCollins hardcover ed. ISBN 0-00-200032-6

Canadian Cataloguing in Publication Data

McCann, Edna
The heritage book 2000

Annual.
2000
Continues: McCann, Edna. Heritage book, ISSN 0711-4737
ISSN 1489-937X
ISBN 0-00-200032-6 (2000 issue)

1. Anecdotes. 2. Devotional calendars. 3. Maxims, English. I. Title
PN6331.M32   242'.2   C99-900610-X

99 00 01 02 03 04 HC 8 7 6 5 4 3 2 1

Printed and bound in the United States

Foreword

My first memory of *The Heritage Book* dates from the summer of 1980. As we prepared to move to Western Canada, a dear neighbour gave us a copy as a farewell gift. She thought that since I was an inspirational writer and poet, we would enjoy something to encourage us on the long journey. The book turned out to be a comfort and companion during late nights and early mornings alike, as the readings prompted the memory of abundant personal experiences that we enjoyed sharing with our two young daughters.

The Heritage Book brought back memories of childhood days and recreated some of the special times that had grown dim over the passing years.

I have since realized that most of us have sayings or quotes we "live by." I believe it would be difficult to find someone who hasn't a thought or two they have written down or memorized—because these things express something vital in our lives.

Over the years these books have been both comfort and inspiration. Inspiration is life, and life is inspiration.

Each month of this *Heritage Book* brings forth a fountain of ideas, each page seems to shine with the uplifting touch we all need, today as always. The purpose of each *Heritage Book* is to encourage, enrich, and ennoble a reader with deep and brilliant jewels, a reward for the time of searching.

Margaret Fishback Powers

Introduction

When I began to put together the *Heritage Book* for the year 2000, I paused for some time to reflect on the many historic events and enormous changes that were part of the last one hundred years.

We saw the tragedy of two World Wars and the deaths of kings, presidents and prime ministers. We endured drought, famine and the Great Depression.

We also witnessed the miracle of flight. Rockets have flown to other planets and man has walked on the moon.

We have seen medical history made with heart transplants and "miracle" drugs that have virtually eliminated many diseases. Our life expectancy has increased by five to seven years.

We have telephones, radios, televisions and computers.

The years past have given us many memories and it is with great anticipation, joy and optimism that I look forward to the new century and the new millenium. For me, it will continue to be the varied challenges and experiences that make each day such a delight.

In a world of change, some things are constant: the love of family and friends, the appreciation of the "little" things that add so much to our daily lives and the knowledge that we enter each day with a new chance for happiness.

As ever, I hope that these stories, quotations, poems and anecdotes will add a bit of pleasure to each day of a very special year.

Edna McCann

January

Saturday January 1

AS we celebrate this first day of the year 2000, I have tried to think of extremely wise or profound resolutions to follow. At my advanced age, profound thoughts seem to be somewhat rare, but I believe I was able to find a few appropriate ideas with which to begin a new year and a new century.

Do not let yourself
Worry when you are doing your best,
Hurry when your success will depend on accuracy,
Believe something is impossible to achieve unless you have tried it,
Waste time on matters over which you have no control,
Imagine that good intentions are an acceptable excuse, or
Waste a day—because time is the most precious gift.

My wish for us all is a year of good health, peace, joy and prosperity. Happy New Year!

Sunday January 2

LET the words of my mouth, and the meditation of my heart, be acceptable in thy sight, O Lord, my strength, and my redeemer.

Psalm 19:14

Monday January 3

WONDERFUL as it is to enjoy our large family gatherings during the holiday season, it is often as pleasant to have our lives return to the quiet and order of "normal" once again.

Time spent in the company of family and friends is unquestionably some of the happiest of the year. However, as I become older and more deaf, I find that the noise and confusion can be somewhat overwhelming. On many occasions I need a few moments of quiet to refresh myself.

Surprisingly, many children who seem to have unlimited energy and endurance also need these times of quiet. It's a wise parent who will allow the children some "down time"—perhaps a chance to read or to be read to, or time for a short nap. Children, as well as adults, are more able to enjoy the festivities if they are rested and refreshed.

Much as they love the holidays, perhaps even children are happy to return to a more regular schedule.

Tuesday January 4

Skaters at Dusk

At the bend of the river the skaters glide
Like swift-winged swallows upon their way.
There where the ice is smooth and wide
They circle and swing, they lean and sway.

The wind dies down with the coming of night;
The purple and crimson afterglow
Is darkly etched with the eager flight
Where the swaying, swinging skaters go.

Their laughter echoes, their voices ring,
Forward and backward they swoop and wheel—
Sharp on the air the zip and zing
Where the ice is cut by the flying steel.

Low in the west a star's clear flame;
The red lit river grows dark at last;
A boy's voice calls another's name—
Already the supper hour is past.

The clank of unloosened skates, the tread
Of tingling feet on the frozen ground,
And hungry as wolves, and ready for bed
The tired skaters are homeward bound.

These words of Grace Noll Crowell came to
mind as I watched our neighbourhood youngsters

trudge home, skates in hand, from a day of skating at our Mill Pond.

Wednesday January 5

WE are never as generous as when we are giving advice.

Duc de la Rochefoucauld

Thursday January 6

TODAY is the celebration of the Epiphany in the Western Church. The word "epiphany" comes from a Greek word that refers to the arrival of the Three Wise Men at Jesus' birth and also to his baptism.

Around the world, people of European extraction will celebrate this day by going to church and enjoying a family feast.

For those of you celebrating today, I offer one of the best-loved hymns.

As With Gladness

As with gladness men of old
Did the guiding star behold,
As with joy they hailed its light
Leading onward, beaming bright;
So, most gracious Lord may we
Evermore be led to thee.

As they offered gifts most rare
At that cradle rude and bare;
So may we with holy joy,
Pure and free from sins alloy
All our costliest treasures bring,
Christ, to thee our heavenly King.

William Chatterton Dix, 1860

Friday January 7

A LOVELY note from one of my readers reminded me of the fun we used to have on many a cold January evening.

Mary wrote from British Columbia, "I can remember the old piano that we had in the corner of the living room. My mother and grandmother (who was living with us) both played beautifully. It was a rare evening when one or the other wouldn't adjust the stool to the right height, and sit down to entertain us by playing our favourite tunes."

Like Mary, I remember the happiness that playing the piano gave to my mother. After dinner, while Father worked on his sermon for the next Sunday, Mother would begin to play, ever so softly at first, and then more loudly as she became wrapped up in the joy of the music. Often we children would leave what we were doing and slip down to sit beside the piano. Mother frequently played her favourite hymns and, because we knew them by heart, we would sing along with great enthusiasm. Soon Father would join in and before we knew it, we would be in a rousing chorus of "The Marching Saints."

Those were wonderful times and I know that we all cherished the evenings and happy family occasions together. I wish that more families today could know the joy of those less hectic times.

Saturday January 8

WINTER moves south across the land, and it's always a fascinating thought to imagine the little electric blanket lights coming on to mark the progress of the cold front.

Bill Vaughan

Sunday January 9

I HAVE set the Lord always before me: because He is at my right hand, I shall not be moved.

Therefore my heart is glad, and my glory rejoiceth: my flesh also shall rest in hope.

Psalm 16:8–9

Monday January 10

WHEN I hear music I fear no danger, I am invulnerable, I see no foe. I am related to the earliest times, and to the latest.

Henry David Thoreau

Tuesday January 11

MOST of us tend to think the use of credit cards to be a fairly recent phenomenon. Although the use of credit cards has ballooned to incredible proportions and there is scarcely a thing left in the world that cannot be bought (or borrowed) on credit, the idea of cash substitutes actually goes back to medieval times.

Knights used their rings, engraved with their coats of arms, as proof of their financial standing. Highway robbers were numerous, and carrying large sums of cash on the wooded trails was dangerous. For this reason, innkeepers would keep a master list of the various seals and signet rings and the peripatetic knights would be billed later. Failure to pay meant that the creditor barred the castle gate until cash was received.

Although the first credit cards were issued in the 1920s by oil companies and department stores, the term "credit card" was coined by Edward Bellamy in his *Looking Backward, 2000–1887*, published in 1888. A man of vision, Bellamy predicted that people would eventually carry a single card. We are nearly there.

Wednesday January 12

THE family is one of nature's masterpieces.

George Santayana

Thursday January 13

NOTHING is more beautiful than one snowflake. Unfortunately they seldom come that way.

Friday January 14

THE ice hockey season is in full swing, and this exciting game continues to become more popular each year. As the National Hockey League expands, fans in many areas of North America are able to enjoy the fast-paced action that the game provides.

Back in 1928, one of the most amazing games in history took place in Montreal. At the time, the New York Rangers were playing the second game of a best-of-three series against the Montreal Maroons (now known as the Canadiens). Lester Patrick, the silver-haired coach and manager of the Rangers, was behind the bench when Lorne Chabot, the Rangers goaltender, suffered a serious eye injury and was taken from the ice to the hospital. In those days, teams did not have a back-up goaltender.

In spite of the fact that he had never before played goal, Patrick donned the pads and put on an inspirational performance for the rest of the game.

His outstanding play allowed his teammates, who were enormous underdogs, to go on and win the game 2–1, tying the series at one game apiece. His feat would go down in the annals of hockey as one of the most courageous displays of its kind.

Saturday January 15

TODAY is the birthday of Dr. Martin Luther King, Jr., the great African-American statesman. The late Dr. King was instrumental in introducing the strategy of non-violent civil disobedience to the black struggle for equality, and turning the struggle into a mass movement.

In his acceptance speech for the Nobel Peace Prize on December 11, 1964, he said, "Non-violence is the answer to the crucial political and moral question of our time: the need for man to overcome oppression and violence without resorting to oppression and violence.

"Man must evolve for all human conflict a method which rejects revenge, aggression and retaliation. The foundation of such method is love."

Dr. King would have been 71 years old today.

Sunday January 16

My Father, for another night
Of quiet sleep and rest,
For all the joy of morning light,
Thy holy name be blest.
Now with the newborn day I give
Myself to answer thee,
That as thou willest I may live
And what thou willest be.

Hymn by Rev. Sir H. W. Baker, 1875

Monday January 17

PERHAPS the most valuable result of all education is the ability to make yourself do the thing you have to do, when it ought to be done, whether you like it or not. It is the first lesson that ought to be learned, and however early a man's training begins, it is probably the last lesson that he learns thoroughly.

Tuesday January 18

PEOPLE are afraid of the future, of the unknown. If a man faces up to it, and takes the dare of the future, he can have some control over his destiny. That's an exciting idea to me, better than waiting with everyone else to see what is going to happen.

John H. Glenn, Jr.

Wednesday January 19

FAR better it is to dare mighty things, to win glorious triumphs even though checkered by failure, than to rank with those poor spirits who neither enjoy much nor suffer much, because they live in the gray twilight that knows not victory nor defeat.

Theodore Roosevelt

Thursday January 20

WINTER is the time for comfort, for good food and warmth, for the touch of a friendly hand and for a talk beside the fire; it is time for the home.

Dame Edith Sitwell

Those of us who experience the onslaught of winter storms might be looking for "good food and warmth" today. I offer our family recipe for Crabmeat Chowder, a true comfort soup.

1 cup canned crabmeat
3 tbsp. butter (or margarine)
2 tbsp. diced onion
3 tbsp. flour
2 cups chicken stock (or tinned chicken broth)
1/2 cup tomato juice
1/8 tsp. cayenne pepper
1/2 tsp. dried hot mustard

1 cup diced potato
1 cup whole milk (scalded)
1 tsp. salt
1 tbsp. finely chopped fresh parsley (or dried flakes)

Drain juice from crabmeat, separate into shreds, set aside. Melt butter in a 5-quart saucepan, add onion and sauté 5 minutes until tender, stirring occasionally. Add flour and, when blended, stir in the stock, tomato juice, cayenne pepper and mustard. Add potatoes and heat to boiling over high heat. Reduce heat to low, cover and simmer 30 minutes longer or until potatoes are tender. Just before serving, add crabmeat, scalded milk, salt and parsley. Serve very hot. Serves 6.

Friday January 21

THE ultimate measure of a man is not where he stands in moments of comfort and convenience, but where he stands at times of challenge and controversy.

Martin Luther King, Jr.

Saturday January 22

WHEN you have closed your doors, and darkened your room, remember never to say that you are alone, for you are not alone; God is within, and your genius is within—and what need have they of light to see what you are doing?

Epictetus

Sunday January 23

WHEN I consider thy heavens, even the work of thy fingers, the moon and the stars, which thou hast ordained;

What is man, that thou art mindful of him, and the son of man, that thou visitest him?

Psalm 8:3–4

Monday January 24

AMERICAN statesman Henry Kissinger once remarked, "The nice thing about being a celebrity is that when you bore people, they think it is their fault."

Tuesday January 25

ACROSS our country and in many places around the world, Scottish clubs and societies will meet this evening in celebration of Burns Night. They will gather to honour "Robbie" Burns, the famous Scottish poet, who was born this day in 1759.

One of the highlights of the evening is always

the procession of kilted men and women, led by a bagpiper, who "pipes in the Haggis" which rests resplendently on a large silver platter.

The master of ceremonies may then recite Burns' famous poem, "To A Haggis," after which he will usually repeat the Selkirk Grace, composed when Burns was a guest of the Earl of Selkirk in Scotland.

Some hae meat and canna eat,
And some wad eat that want it:
But we hae meat and we can eat,
And sae the Lord be thankit.

It will be an evening of great pomp, ceremony and good fun for our Scottish friends.

Wednesday January 26

MY dear friend, Emily, a native of Philadelphia, has a great grandson who is a medical student. He is presently working in obstetrics and seems particularly enthusiastic about this area of medicine. When Emily asked Jason about his love of obstetrics, she laughed when she heard his reply.

"Gran, when I was on the different medical rotations, I developed symptoms for almost everything that I was treating. I suffered from a heart attack, asthma, lung cancer and appendicitis. In the emergency ward, I could hardly keep up with my symptoms. Finally, I can relax. I know I won't be having a baby."

Thursday January 27

WE would be wise to remember that failure is temporary—but so is success!

Friday January 28

THE most unhappy person on earth is the one who rises in the morning with nothing to do and wonders how to pass the day.

Saturday January 29

ISN'T it amazing how the winter weather has a way of drawing the youngsters outdoors to play, while the old folks are chased, shivering, inside to warm ourselves by the fire.

I enjoyed looking out the window today as the neighbourhood children played exuberantly in the fresh snowfall. Little Christine, a six-year-old from down the street, knocked on our door to ask if I wanted to come outside and make angels with her. I demurred, but promised I would watch her from the window, and then I invited her to join me for hot chocolate when she was finished.

Christine is one of those delightful children

who is comfortable with youngsters and adults alike. She happily made about a dozen angels on our lawn before joining me for hot chocolate and cookies. She chatted gaily about her love of snow and all things associated with winter. When it was time to go home, she announced that the hot chocolate was "delicious" and the cookies were the "best ones I ever ate."

In an age when not all children are so well mannered, I'm sure that Christine's parents must be delighted to have such a polite, unspoiled and charming daughter. As a senior citizen, I appreciate very much the time I am able to spend with such a lovely child.

Sunday January 30

GOD is our refuge and strength, a very present help in trouble. Therefore will not we fear, though the earth be removed, and though the mountains be carried into the midst of the sea;

Though the waters thereof roar and be troubled, though the mountains shake with the swelling thereof. The Lord of Hosts is with us; the God of Jacob is our refuge.

Psalm 46:1–3, 11

Monday January 31

IFOUND it interesting to learn that Charles Schultz, the creator of "Peanuts," had his cartoons rejected by the staff of his high-school yearbook. He took a correspondence course in cartoon drawing, then applied for a cartoonist's job at Walt Disney Studios. He was rejected.

How lucky for all of us who have grown to love Charlie Brown, his dog, Snoopy, and the rest of the characters in his world-famous "Peanuts" cartoon, that Schultz persevered.

You don't have to be a genius, you don't need enormous talent; you just have to keep plugging away.

February

Tuesday February 1

February

The fields are bedded down with snow
Like blankets tucked about their ears,
As if the world has gone to sleep.
But now and then a bush appears
Wearing a crown of purest gems,
With scarlet berries on white stems.
The windbreak running to the lake
Has heavy trunks like silver birch;
Even the weeds have hoods of snow,
Like quaint old women in a church.
The hens have frosted beards and look
Like old men in a picture book.
Along the highway muffled wheels
Go by without a breath of sound.
The fence posts stand like sentinels
Wearing tall helmets diamond crowned;
The mailman in his battered truck
Has drifted snow and ice to buck.
And yet I know that spring is nigh
Although the wind is cold and raw;
The sky is softer than it was
The fields have started in to thaw,

Putting aside the winter dress
To don their springtime loveliness.

Edna Jaques

Wednesday February 2

FEBRUARY 2 is celebrated in many ways, but here in North America, the most amusing is known as Groundhog Day.

This verse explains how these little forecasters judge the outcome of winter.

Out from his burrow in the ground,
Softly (you cannot hear his sound),
The groundhog comes, so people say,
On February's second day.
And then he looks around with care
To see if his own shadow's there,
Lying beside him on the snow.
And if it is, back he will go,
And six weeks more he will abide
In the warm hole where he doth hide.

Author unknown

Thursday February 3

PEACE comes not from the absence of conflict in life, but from the ability to cope with it.

Author unknown

Friday February 4

THE error of youth is to believe that intelligence is a substitute for experience, while the error of age is to believe that experience is a substitute for intelligence.

Author unknown

Saturday February 5

"IF I had my life to live over again I would..." How often we hear that said, or perhaps even say it ourselves.

As I look back, I realize that there are very few things I would, or could, have changed. As the days, months and years flow by, we adjust our actions and our plans as the conditions demand. Our judgements are based on our experience and our moral standards, but some of life's pattern is also the result of forces over which we have no control.

However, if we are not pleased with what we see of our past, and there are things that we could change, it is never too late to start a life that will be more satisfactory to us. We cannot redo the past, but we can find happiness in a new way, appreciating the many opportunities that are presented to us in this wonderful world.

"All of life is more or less what the French would call *s'imposer*—to be able to create one's terms for what one does."

Kenneth Tynan

Sunday February 6

RELIGION is a multicoloured lantern. Everyone looks through a particular colour, but the candle is always there.

Author unknown

Monday February 7

IN case you're worried about what's going to become of the younger generation, it's going to grow up and start worrying about the younger generation.

Roger Allen

Tuesday February 8

THERE are times in every life when friends or loved ones pass away. We miss them terribly. The thought that we shall never see them again could burden us with hopelessness and grief.

Although it may be difficult to do, we need to remember that we still have their influence about us; we can still use the inspiration that came from them. We can consider the great privilege of having had time to spend together, and feel about us the spirit that we receive from them. If we are able to think in this way, perhaps we can turn our sense of loss into an unselfish hope that our lives may be better for all that we received from them.

Beautiful memories are wonderful things,
They last till the longest day.
They never wear out, they never get lost
And can never be given away.
To some you may be forgotten,
To others a thing of the past,
But to those who loved and lost you
Your memory will always last.

Author unknown

Wednesday February 9

THE brilliant playwright, George Bernard Shaw, had a wonderful sense of humour.

One day he received an invitation from a lady who was well known as a celebrity chaser. It read, "Lady ———— will be at home Thursday between the hours of four and six."

Mr. Shaw returned her card with the following message.

"Mr. Shaw likewise."

Thursday February 10

SOME people treat life like a slot machine, trying to put in as little as possible and hoping to hit the jackpot. Wiser people think of life as an investment from which they receive in terms of what they put in.

Author unknown

Friday February 11

WE love old cathedrals, old furniture and old prints, but we have already forgotten about the beauty of old men. I think an appreciation of that kind of beauty is essential to our life; for beauty, it seems to me, is what is old and mellow and well smoked.

Lin Yutang

Saturday February 12

MY good friend, Jake Frampton, stopped in for dinner this evening. My former readers will remember that Jake owns a small used bookstore and he regularly spoils me by bringing books for me to enjoy. This evening was no exception.

Jake knows that I like to read books of all types, but that mysteries are particular favourites. Dick Francis, Mary Higgins Clark, Lawrence Sanders and Robin Cook are all authors whose works send chills up and down my spine. The author whose writing I will soon enjoy is Ann Rule, a writer whose works are new to me.

A former Seattle policewoman, Ms. Rule is the author of many *New York Times* bestsellers. Several of her works are Crime File Volumes and one of them, *The Stranger Beside Me*, is her own account of her horror at finding that her friend and co-worker, Ted Bundy, was a serial killer.

The book that Jake brought for me is Ms. Rule's first attempt at a novel. It is described as a "riveting tale of psychological suspense," and I look forward to many hours of reading pleasure.

It is my hope that Jake will feel that a home-cooked meal will be fitting thanks for his kindness.

Sunday February 13

I F I take the wings of the morning, and dwell in the uttermost parts of the sea; even there shall thy hand lead me, and thy right hand shall hold me.

Psalm 139:9–10

Monday February 14

Valentine's Day

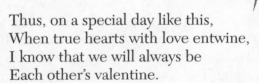

Between your heart and my heart
There is a bond unbroken;
Though time and mile divide us
And words remain unspoken.

Thus, on a special day like this,
When true hearts with love entwine,
I know that we will always be
Each other's valentine.

Hearts like ours do not forget,

This bond we cannot sever.
Within your heart and my heart
We'll be Valentines forever.

Author unknown

These lovely words were a part of a Valentine's card from my husband, George, so many years ago. Although he passed away far too early, my heart still feels the unbroken bond between us—on Valentine's Day and all the other days of the year too.

Tuesday February 15

ONE of our neighbours is a flight attendant with Air Canada. She regularly flies to Paris and several other European destinations but, air travel being what it is today, she is rarely away for more than a few days at a time. Her duties during a flight are many and varied, but they are also quite different from those of the original attendants (known then as stewardesses).

It was on May 15, 1930 that the first stewardesses boarded planes, and their flight manuals contained these instructions:

Keep the clock and altimeter wound.

Carry a railroad timetable in case the plane is grounded.

Warn passengers against throwing their cigars

and cigarettes out the windows.

Keep an eye on passengers when they go to the lavatory to be sure that they don't mistakenly go out the emergency exit.

How courageous those young women must have been!

Wednesday February 16

LOVE does not consist of gazing at each other, but in looking outward together in the same direction.

Antoine de Saint-Exupéry

Thursday February 17

THIS is the time of year when many northerners pack up and head for the sunny south. Marg's friend Joyce told us of her first trip to Florida, when she was just a youngster.

"My parents were proud new owners of a Studebaker convertible and, anxious to give it a real test, had decided to visit with Mom's cousins who lived in Palm Beach. My grandparents were also invited, but Dad was having some difficulty persuading Grandpa that he would be comfortable riding in a 'ragtop' car. Grandpa had convinced himself that a convertible couldn't possibly be kept warm and, as the drive south included a number of very cold states, he wasn't sure that he was willing to risk it. Finally, however, my grandmother's powers of persuasion won him over and we prepared to depart.

"Grandpa dressed for the voyage as if he were travelling with Admiral Byrd to the South Pole. Long underwear, heavy pants, flannel shirt, coat, scarf and hat—grandpa was wearing them all. He didn't know that Dad had rigged some form of hose to run the heat directly into the back seat and was about to pump there every bit of heat the car could produce.

"Dad kept a close eye on the rear-view mirror and asked frequently, 'Warm enough Bert?' Grandpa deserved great credit. He was able to reply, 'Not so bad, Neal.' (This despite the beads of sweat that rolled down his face and disappeared into the scarf which hugged his neck so warmly.)

"I was also in the back seat complaining loudly, 'Daddy, I'm boiling!' By the time we reached Pennsylvania, I had stripped down to my underwear. It was a long, hot trip."

Friday February 18

THERE is in every true woman's heart a spark of heavenly fire, which lies dormant in the broad daylight of propriety, but which kindles up and beams and blazes in the dark hours of adversity.

Washington Irving

Saturday February 19

FINISH every day and be done with it. You have done what you could. Some blunders and absurdities no doubt crept in; forget them as soon as you can. Tomorrow is a new day; begin it well and serenely and with too high a spirit to be cumbered with your old nonsense. This day is too dear, with its hopes and invitations, to waste a moment on the yesterdays.

Ralph Waldo Emerson

Sunday February 20

IN all thy ways acknowledge him, and he shall direct thy paths.

Proverbs 3:6

Monday February 21

SMILE at each other, smile at your wife, smile at your husband, smile at your children, smile at each other—it doesn't matter who it is—and that will help you grow up in greater love for each other.

Mother Teresa

I was reminded of these wise words as I sat in the food court of our local mall. Seated at the table nearby was a young man who was eating lunch alone, and whose demeanor suggested that he was angry. He was a good-looking fellow, and as I studied him, I was thinking to myself that he could be strikingly handsome if only he would smile. He caught me looking at him and asked, in an unfriendly way, "What are you staring at?"

Embarrassed, I began an apology—then changed my mind. "I was thinking that you would be so handsome if only you would smile!" It was his turn to be embarrassed, and then he turned on a dazzling smile that lit up his face.

"Why thank you," he said. "You've made my day a whole lot better."

Tuesday February 22

EVERY material goal, even if it is met, will pass away. But the heritage of our children is timeless. Our children are our messengers to the future.

Billy Graham

Wednesday February 23

If you sit down at set of sun
And count the acts that you have done,
And, counting find

One self denying deed, one word
That eased the heart of him who heard—
One glance most kind,
That fell like sunshine where it went—
Then you may count the day well spent.

George Eliot

Thursday February 24

AUTHOR William Saroyan, who died of cancer in May, 1981, once wrote "The best part of a person stays forever."

Shortly before his death, he phoned Associated Press to report that the disease had spread to several of his vital organs. At that time, he left with reporters his final statement, to be used after his death. "Everybody has got to die, but I always thought that an exception would be made in my case. Now what?"

Friday February 25

CHANGE, for the better or for the worse, is not something that I deal with in an expert manner. I really am a creature of habit and anything that upsets my routine is not usually very welcome in my life. People from the past and the present have expressed interesting reflections on change, and I offer several of their thoughts to you today.

Change is the law of life. And those who look only at the past or the present are certain to miss the future.

John F. Kennedy

Weep not that the world changes—did it keep a stable, changeless state, 'twere cause indeed to weep.

William Cullen Bryant

Nothing is permanent but change.

Heraclitus (500 B.C.)

All changes, even the most longed for, have their melancholy, for what we leave behind us is a part of ourselves; we must die to one life before we can enter another.

Anatole France

A permanent state of transition is man's most noble condition.

Juan Ramón Jiménez

Saturday February 26

MY daughter Marg and I visited some friends in our local nursing home. The severe cold and wintry weather is particularly hard on shut-ins or residents of nursing homes,

as it often means that they are confined indoors
for weeks at a time.

This poem, framed and hanging on the wall, is
an important reminder to us all.

My aged head lifts and turns toward the hall.
Could it be that someone is paying me a call?
Footsteps draw near, hope stirs anew,
Who could it be? Friends left are so few.
A strand of loose hair is tucked quickly in place,
My dress smoothed out; steps slow in pace.
A woman comes in; the room fills with perfume,
"Oh I'm so sorry—I have the wrong room.
Miss Stone, do you know her?"
"Yes dear, in room four."
Slightly embarrassed, she goes out the door.
My tired heart aches, hands grip the chair;
The clock seems to tick..."no one to care."
Christmas and Easter, people come through
Distributing gifts, handmade and new.
Then, soon forgotten, until the next year,
No one remembers that I reside here.
Patients pass on. Then daughters and sons
Say in the halls, "I did mean to come."
Dear God...Dear God...Please let it be
That one will remember and come visit me.

Eleanor Bleakley

Sunday February 27

THE sabbath was made for man, and not man for the sabbath.

Mark 2:27

Monday February 28

A FRIEND of mine confided that growing older confronts you with two great shocks.

"One is the first time you are asked if you should receive the senior citizen's discount. The second is the first time that no one asks if you get the senior's discount—it has been assumed."

Tuesday February 29

FOR any of you whose birthday is today, this is your one year in four to celebrate. As you get older, you will probably be pleased not to have so many birthdays.

Yet age doesn't count too much in life's span. Some people age early, while others never seem to lose the sparkle in their eye and the spring in their step. It is the way that you feel and act that determines your enjoyment in life. Those who grow old gracefully seem to get more pleasure out of life than those who count the years.

Being born on February 29 gives you an extra reward in life. Delight in it! This day is really a "bonus" day for everyone—a day to make the most of and enjoy.

March

Wednesday March 1

FOR our friends of Welsh descent, today is celebrated as St. David's Day. There are several interesting legends associated with this celebration. It is said that daffodils burst into bloom on this day to honour the man who was the sixth-century leader of the church. On the Sunday nearest to St. David's Day vases and pots of daffodils decorate the churches, and strains of the old hymn "Men of Harleck," sung in the native Welsh tongue, are heard wherever Welshmen gather to worship.

Another legend suggests that the Welsh won a victory over their Saxon enemies by having the Welshmen wear leeks in their hats so that they could recognize, and not kill, their own men.

Here in Canada, and around the world, people of Welsh ancestry wear a leek in their hatband and a daffodil in their lapel today.

Although my heritage is a mix of Scottish and Irish, I would like to think that I could claim a bit of Welsh as well. I think that it would explain two of my characteristics that I associate with the Welsh—namely, tenaciousness and puritanism.

To all Welshmen, wherever you are, enjoy your wonderful heritage on this St. David's Day.

Thursday March 2

THIS is a story I love and my fond readers will forgive me for repeating.

Three-year-old Louis spent many hours playing in his father's saddle-making shop in the French village of Coupvray.

One day the little boy quietly picked up two of his father's sharp awls and left the shop. As he hurried along the cobblestone walk, he tripped, fell, and was struck in the eyes by the awls. At that moment, Louis Braille became totally blind.

When he was ten years old, his parents sent him to the school for the blind in Paris. The school's founder, Valentin Huay, had invented a system to enable blind people to "read" with their fingers by using cut-out letters of cloth pasted on pages of paper. However, each letter was enormous and the whole process was time consuming and impractical.

In 1836, when Louis was 27 years old, he finally perfected his own system of raised dots and dashes that was to make up the "Braille" alphabet allowing sightless people around the world to read and write.

Isn't it ironic that Louis used an awl to create his own alphabet? The very same instrument that had caused Louis Braille's blindness became the implement of his gift to the sightless.

Friday March 3

YOU must give some time to your fellow men. Even if it's a little thing, do something for others—something for which you get no pay but the privilege of doing it.

Albert Schweitzer

Saturday March 4

Home is the habit you've never quite broken,
Home is the hearth where you warm your soul,
When everything 'round you is coming to
    pieces,
Home is the place where your heart can
    feel whole.

Shelly Miller

Sunday March 5

TEACH me, good Lord, to serve thee as thou deservest, to give and not to count the cost— to fight and not to heed the wounds—to toil and not to seek for rest—to labour and not to ask for any reward, save that of knowing that we do thy will through Jesus Christ our Lord.

Ignatius Loyola

Monday March 6

AS we drove past the high school the other day, I was quite surprised to see a large number of students smoking. I was even more shocked when my son-in-law Bruce told me that teenagers now make up the largest number of smokers. Bruce also told me that statistics show that nearly 70 percent of children 16 years of age and under have tried a cigarette at least once.

Somehow I assumed that because of the anti-smoking lessons taught in schools, these youngsters would understand the seriousness of the health issues involved in smoking.

I wonder if a visit to the hospital to see those who suffer from lung cancer and emphysema, and for whom every breath is a struggle, might have a greater impact?

Young people feel invincible, but how I wish that they would understand the grave consequences of smoking.

Tuesday March 7

TOMORROW is Ash Wednesday, the first day of Lent. Although few people adhere to the Lenten ritual of fasting, I feel it is an important part of our religion. Just as Jesus sacrificed for 40 days in the wilderness, so should we honour him with a sacrifice of our own.

Wednesday March 8

A NUMBER of us "old folks" were enjoying a meal together when a friend, Martha, posed a most thought provoking question.

"What do you think is the most important thing that a parent gives to their child?"

After much discussion, the six of us around the dinner table came up with these ideas.

Children need to believe in themselves, and they will achieve whatever they think they can achieve. When children believe in their abilities, their energies may be used to work toward their goals. What children believe about themselves comes directly from parents, and, whether they know it or not, this influence is ongoing, maybe for a lifetime.

Children need a strong sense of security and with that security will come the ability and willingness to think, to express opinions and to be open to others' thoughts and opinions. We feel that this will also lead to the formation of strong friendships, for an open mind is needed to form the strong bonds and the friendships that so enrich all of our lives.

All children need a firm grasp of the importance of honesty and integrity. How better to see this than watching how we, as parents, deal with issues in our own lives. We should expect no more of our children than we show them of ourselves.

Unconditional love is the key to happiness.

Love is something that children must see and live with.

How cherished is the home where the family is valued, and everyone knows he belongs.

Thursday March 9

MY grandson Marshall, a lawyer, recently attended a banquet where he was seated next to a very elderly barrister and his wife. As the toastmaster rose to get the evening program under way, Marshall leaned over and whispered to his venerable neighbour, "May I pour you some coffee, sir?"

"Good heavens, no," replied the elderly gentleman. "It might keep me awake through the speeches."

Friday March 10

When the sun shines on a winter day
I dream about the spring,
With all the wondrous happy joys
That April days can bring.
I soon forget the cold, cold winds
The heavy winter snow...
My heart is on a springtime cloud,
The world takes on a glow.

Author unknown

How happy I am that spring is just around the corner!

Saturday March 11

ARTHUR Gordon, in his book *A Touch of Wonder*, wrote:

" 'There is not enough darkness in all the world to put out the light of one small candle.'

This inscription was found on a small new gravestone after a devastating air raid on Britain in World War II.

In moments of discouragement, defeat or even despair, there are always certain things to cling to. Little things usually: remembered laughter, the face of a sleeping child, a tree in the wind— in fact, any reminder of something deeply felt or dearly loved.

No man is so poor as not to have many of these small candles. When they are lighted, darkness goes away—and a touch of wonder remains."

Sunday March 12

Doubt sees the obstacles,
Faith sees the way;
Doubt sees the blackest night,
Faith sees the day;
Doubt dreads to take a step,

Faith soars on high;
Doubt questions, "Who believes?"
Faith answers, "I!"

Author unknown

Monday March 13

"THE nicest and sweetest days are not those on which anything very splendid or wonderful or exciting happens, but just those that bring simple pleasures, following one another softly, like pearls slipping off a string."

These words from Lucy Maud Montgomery, found in her book *Anne of Avonlea*, describe my day perfectly.

Early in the morning, while having my tea in the sunroom, two bright red cardinals came to the feeder outside my windows. Their brilliant colour looked like fire against the snow.

Later in the morning, our local librarian called to say that the book I was waiting for had come in.

I enjoyed lunch with Lila, a very dear old friend whose company is such a comfort to me.

Then my son-in-law Bruce surprised me with a pot of tulips and my great-grandson Mickey called from his dorm at university just to tell me that he missed me.

These simple things made a day of pearls for me, and I hope it was the same for you.

Tuesday March 14

SPRINGTIME is the land awakening. The March winds are the morning yawn.

Author unknown

Wednesday March 15

ALTHOUGH spring is just a week away, our weather doesn't feel very spring-like. As I looked out on the icy garden this morning, I remembered a delightful "rite of spring" in the British Columbia city of Victoria. Located on Vancouver Island, Victoria has a very temperate climate, and often enjoys the warm temperatures of spring earlier than the rest of Canada. One week early in March is announced as "Flower Counting Week." During this week, residents of the city, both young and old, go into their gardens or into gardens in parks and other public areas, and count the number of flowers that they see. So popular has this ritual become that schools now give students and teachers an hour off to participate in the tallying of crocuses, daffodils, tulips and any other spring flowers.

As flowers are counted, the numbers are phoned in to a Flower Count Centre and the grand total is announced daily on the radio and the television.

For several years now, our local television station has picked up coverage of this event.

Each year I find it more and more difficult not to be pea-green with envy as I see people in shirt sleeves or light jackets wandering about in a garden that is in bloom, while we look out on lingering snow.

Thursday March 16

MY grandson Fred and his wife, June, celebrated their wedding anniversary today. A good friend offered this tribute to the happy marriage that Fred and June have built over the years.

"Building a good marriage and building a good log fire are similar in many ways. You build a fire with paper and it goes up in a blaze. Then the blaze burns down and you wonder if the fire will fizzle out. You blow on it and fan it for all you are worth. Sometimes smoke almost chokes you, but if the materials are good and if you invest enough energy and interest in maintaining it, soon the logs will catch, and your fire takes on new qualities."

Friday March 17

TODAY my mind turns, not so much to St. Patrick, the patron saint of Ireland, but to my many Irish friends whom I have known and cherished.

Two qualities make the Irish very special to me. The one is their profound sense of loyalty to homeland and friends; the other is the strength of family ties.

I am proud, on St. Patrick's Day, to be able to claim an Irish background on my father's side, and it's glad I'll be to be "wearin' o' the green" today.

O Ireland, isn't it grand you look—
Like a bride in her rich adornin'
And with all the pent-up love of my heart
I bid you top o' the mornin'.

John Locke

Saturday March 18

When good friends walk beside us
On the trails that we must keep,
Our burdens seem less heavy
And the hills are not so steep.
The weary miles pass swiftly
Taken in joyous stride,
And all the world seems brighter
When friends walk by your side.

Author unknown

Sunday March 19

ALMIGHTY God, who seest that we have no power of ourselves to help ourselves; Keep us both outwardly in our bodies, and inwardly in our souls; that we may be defended from all adversities which may happen to the body, and from all evil thoughts which may assault and hurt the soul; through Jesus Christ our Lord. Amen.

Collect for the 2nd Sunday in Lent

Monday March 20

THE kind of world that we live in tomorrow depends—not partially, but entirely—upon the type and quality of our children's education today.

It is our responsibility, as adults, to be sure that every child receives the best education possible. Remember, our children are our future.

Tuesday March 21

TODAY is the first day of spring and I, for one, welcome the season with open arms (actually it was with open windows). Longfellow once wrote the following about spring:

"If spring came but once a century instead of once a year, or burst forth with the sound of an earthquake, and not in silence, what wonder and expectation there would be in all hearts to behold the miraculous change! But now the silent succession suggests nothing but necessity. To most men only the cessation of the miracle would be miraculous, and the perpetual exercise of God's power seems less wonderful than the withdrawal would be."

Wednesday March 22

I ENJOY this story. I hope you will, too.

A very elderly lady had lived a long and healthy life on a farm in the northern United States. The only real problem she ever encountered was an injury to her hand in a corn picker when she was 12 years old. Then, 86 years later, she slipped in the barn and broke her arm.

Ordinarily a very cheerful person, she became somewhat fretful and complained, "Gee, everything happens to me. First it was my hand, and now it's my arm."

Thursday March 23

ADVICE is what we ask for when we already know the answer—but wish we didn't.

Friday March 24

I AM one of those people who really enjoys eating a hearty breakfast. I feel that I am healthier because of this regimen and research seems to be on my side in this thought.

Researchers have found that people who eat breakfast consume more essential nutrients, including calcium, fibre and vitamins C, B1, and B2, than people who skip this meal. Usually better nutrition means better resistance to infection.

One study suggests that people who eat breakfast may live longer than those who don't. Of course breakfast lovers may simply be more likely to stay in shape than breakfast skippers.

Another very important study indicates that children score better on tests when they have had a good morning meal. Having a good breakfast doesn't make students more intelligent, but it does increase their attention span, allowing greater learning to take place.

As well, people who choose not to eat breakfast have a metabolic rate that is four to five percent below normal. This means that of two people who have the same caloric intake in a day, the one who doesn't eat breakfast could gain eight pounds per year.

A big plus for us seniors is that many restaurants offer reasonably priced breakfast specials. We can enjoy good company while improving our health.

Saturday March 25

REFLECT upon your present blessings, of which every man has many; not on your past misfortunes, of which all men have some.

Charles Dickens

Sunday March 26

WE beseech thee, Almighty God, look upon the hearty desires of thy humble servants, and stretch forth the right hand of thy Majesty, to be our defence against all our enemies; through Jesus Christ our Lord. Amen.

Collect for the 3rd Sunday in Lent

Monday March 27

HOW far you go in life depends on your being tender with the young, compassionate with the aged, and tolerant of the weak and the strong—because someday you will have been all of these.

George Washington Carver

Tuesday March 28

FAITH is believing in things when common sense tells you not to.

Author unknown

Wednesday March 29

A MAN would do well to carry a pencil in his pocket and write down the thoughts of the moment. Those that come unsought are commonly the most valuable and should be secured, because they seldom return.

Francis Bacon

Thursday March 30

L ONG before the Europeans came to North America, the aboriginal people collected the sap from the sugar maple trees.

Legend has it that a woman asked her husband to fill a pot with water. She placed the container at the base of a tree and returned to the wigwam. The husband, angry at being asked to perform such a menial chore, hacked at the tree with the axe he was carrying and turned away. When his wife brought back the pot, she found it filled with liquid, which she mistook for water. She cooked a chunk of venison with what we now know was syrup, and the meat was delicious. Maple syrup has come to be known as a delectable sweet treat associated with the spring season. My mouth waters with the thought.

Friday March 31

H AVE you ever noticed that some people suffer in silence louder than others?

Author unknown

April

Saturday April 1

> The first day of April, some do say,
> Is set apart for All Fools Day.
> But why the people call it so,
> Not I, nor they themselves do know.
> But on this day are people sent,
> On purpose of pure merriment.

> *Poor Robin's Almanac*

I wonder how many readers know that April Fool's Day was celebrated in France more than 400 years ago? As the sun is leaving the zodiac sign of Pisces ("the fish"), the French refer to this day as *Poisson d'avril*.

Although no one is quite sure how it originated, April Fool's Day is a time for playing harmless tricks, sending people on false errands or trying to make them believe ridiculous stories.

In the words of Mark Twain, "The first of April is the day we remember what we are the other 364 days of the year."

Sunday April 2

GRANT, we beseech thee, Almighty God, that we, who for our evil deeds do worthily deserve to be punished, by the comfort of thy grace may mercifully be relieved; through our Lord and Saviour Jesus Christ. Amen.

Collect for the 4th Sunday of Lent

Monday April 3

Is anyone happier because you passed this way?
Does anyone remember that you spoke to him today?
Can you say tonight, in parting with the day that's slipping fast,
That you helped a single brother of the many that you passed?
Is a single heart rejoicing over what you did or said?
Does the man whose hopes were fading, now with courage look ahead?
As you close your eyes in slumber, do you think that God will say,
"You have earned one more tomorrow by the work you did today"?

Author unknown

Tuesday April 4

AH, but a man's reach should exceed his grasp or what's a heaven for?

Robert Browning

Wednesday April 5

OH, how I love the spring! After the long dreary days of winter, the arrival of this wonderful season of renewal lifts my spirits as little else can. Many writers, much more eloquent than I, write of this new beginning.

Our Lord has written the promise of the resurrection not in book alone, but in every leaf of springtime.

Martin Luther

Close to my heart I fold each lovely thing
The sweet day yields; and not disconsolate,
With the calm patience of the woods I wait
For leaf and blossom when God gives us
spring.

John Greenleaf Whittier

Morning dew on roses,
Nature reigns supreme;
Surely this is heaven—
But we call it spring.

Helen Keller

Spring unlocks the flowers to paint the laughing soil.

Reginald Heber

Thursday April 6

GRANDMAS shed the yoke of responsibility, relax and enjoy grandchildren in a way that was not possible when they were raising their own children. And they can glow in the realization that their seed of life will harvest generations to come.

Erma Bombeck

Friday April 7

I BELIEVE this little story may be classified as one of the "what will they think of next?" types.

In a recent letter my friend Marcia, a resident in Boston, Massachusetts, wrote: "Edna, I have just received my flower garden in the mail—and I don't mean in seed packets.

"I ordered 'seed mats' that will give me bright, beautiful flowers all summer long. The biodegradable mats are 8 inches × 30 inches with four in each package, enough to cover 10 square feet. All that I have to do is lay the mats in a sunny spot, cover them lightly with some topsoil, and water regularly. What a wonderfully easy way to garden! According to the directions, the more flowers I cut, the more blossoms will grow, so that I will be able to fill my house with bouquets of cut flowers all summer long."

I will be anxious to hear how Marcia's instant garden grows.

Saturday April 8

An April Day

Take a dozen little clouds,
And a patch of blue;
Take a million raindrops,
As many sunbeams too;
Take a host of violets,
A wandering little breeze;
And myriads of little leaves
Dancing on the trees.
Then mix them all together
In the very quickest way—
Showers, sunshine, birds, flowers
And you'll have an April day.

Author unknown

Sunday April 9

WE beseech thee, Almighty God, mercifully to look upon thy people; that by thy great goodness they may be governed and preserved evermore, both in body and soul; through Jesus Christ our Lord. Amen.

Collect for the 5th Sunday in Lent

Monday April 10

THE worst insult to our elders and betters is to lump them all together as the old, as if they were suffering from some unmentionable disease. We are all suffering from that same disease. It is called life.

Phillip Howard

Tuesday April 11

THIS story was told to me by my son-in-law John. As a lover of the symphony, it gave me chills.

In Prague, Czechoslovakia, it is a tradition that the Spring Festival ends with the performance of Beethoven's Ninth Symphony. In 1963, the brilliant conductor Zubin Mehta was asked to perform with the Czech Philharmonic in the Cathedral of St. Vitus. The church filled with the city's dignitaries and diplomats. Behind them stood nearly 8,000 people. As he was about to begin, one of the festival's directors reminded Mehta that there would be no applause. It is against tradition to applaud in church.

Rehearsals had not gone well, and Mehta, who was conducting this symphony for the first time, needed all of his professional poise if the presentation was to go well.

By the time he had led the musicians into the final "Freude, Schoner Gotterfunken," he knew that it had been a triumph. In the silence that followed as the audience filed out, he felt a wonderful sense of accomplishment—even without the ovation.

Mehta went to his waiting car and, as the car came to the front of the cathedral, he was greeted by an incredible sight. The 8,000 members of the audience, including the dignitaries, were lining both sides of the street and applauding and cheering wildly. Mehta waved until the crowd passed out of sight. Then he put his head back on the seat and wept.

Wednesday April 12

PEOPLE are like stained-glass windows. They glow and sparkle when it is sunny and bright; but when the sun goes down their true beauty is revealed only if there is light from within.

Author unknown

Thursday April 13

WITH small means; to seek elegance rather than luxury, and refinement rather than fashion; to be worthy, not respectable; and wealthy not rich; to listen to stars and birds, to babes and sages, with open heart; to bear all cheerfully, do all bravely, await occasions, hurry never; in a word let the spiritual, unbidden and

unconscious, grow up through the common—
this is to be my symphony.

William Henry Channing

Friday April 14

God, give me sympathy and sense,
And help to keep my courage high;
God, give me calm and confidence,
And, please, a twinkle in my eye.

Margaret Bailey

Saturday April 15

THE happiest people don't necessarily have
the best of everything; they just make the
best of everything.

Sunday April 16

Palm Sunday

FOR those of us of the Christian faith, the
Easter celebration is the basis of our religion—belief in the life to come after death.

The celebration of Easter actually begins
today, Palm Sunday, the week before Easter.
Palm Sunday commemorates Christ's triumphal
entry into Jerusalem. As he rode into the city,

throngs of people ran before him shouting "Hosanna" and waving branches of palm trees.

Long ago, the Palm Sunday ceremony was a sort of religious pageant. In the Roman Catholic Church, the Holy City was reproduced by a priest riding a donkey, leading a procession to the church while parishioners scattered branches and flowers before him.

As a Christian, I believe in the life hereafter, and two of the most powerful verses in the scripture for me are: "Let not your heart be troubled: ye believe in God, believe also in me. In my Father's house are many mansions: if it were not so, I would have told you. I go to prepare a place for you."

John 14:1–2

Monday April 17

IN this spring season, many of us feel a great urge to clean up, repaint, repair and redecorate our homes. Perhaps it is the "nesting instinct," but whatever the cause, my daughter Julia caught the cleaning fever this weekend and, as a result, she has a sparkling clean kitchen. She even managed to get some help, because she convinced her sisters, Marg and Mary, to join in her endeavour.

Using some tips that Julia garnered from magazines, the girls painted the ceiling a beautiful sky blue, then added sponged-on white clouds. This is supposed to open up a small kitchen and make you feel as if there is a sky above you. Next, the cabinets were repainted a sparkling white—guaranteed to brighten even the darkest room. Colourful new knobs and matching coloured fabric on the chairs also added a special decorative touch.

Julia also put up a pine shelf on which she now displays decorative plates, cookie cutters and a few other interesting utensils.

Marg and Mary hung the colourful new mini-blinds and placed the attractive pots of herbs on the window ledge.

It was a lot of work but the results were well worth the effort. The nicest thing was that the girls spent a wonderful day together—and Julia's kitchen is beautiful.

Tuesday April 18

DELORES Garcia described my feelings exactly when she said, "I am rich with years, a millionaire! I have been part of my own generation, then I watched my children's generation grow up, then my grandchildren's, and now my great-grandchildren's."

Wednesday April 19

MY daughter Marg and I do volunteer work in our local public school. I have enormous respect for our teachers and the difficult job that they do so well. I enjoy seeing how each teacher handles the discipline of the students. Every teacher seems to have his or her special tricks that keep order in the classroom.

In 1902, Arthur Benson, an experienced schoolmaster, put into words what should probably be written on the certificate of every new teacher.

"The power of maintaining discipline is the 'unum necessarium' for a teacher; if he has not got it and cannot acquire it, he had better sweep a crossing. It insults the soul, it is destructive of all self-respect and dignity to be incessantly at the mercy of the boys. They are merciless, and the pathos of the situation never touches them at all."

A teacher who is really interested in children will do well whatever the difficulties. One who is not will not do well no matter how favourable the conditions.

Thursday April 20

IF it weren't for the last minute, a lot of things would never get done.

Friday April 21

Good Friday

MY God, my God, why has Thou forsaken me?

Matthew 27:46

Saturday April 22

OUR family has a delicious recipe for a special Easter Egg Lasagna. Although we like to have this appetizing dish on Easter weekend, some of our friends use the hard-boiled eggs that have been left over from the Easter bunny later in the week.

- 1 can (10 oz.) condensed cream of chicken soup
- 1 3/4 cup milk
- 16 oz. low-fat cottage cheese or low-fat ricotta cheese
- 1 box (10 oz.) frozen spinach, thawed, squeezed dry and chopped
- 1/2 cup Parmesan cheese, grated
- 1/4 cup scallions, sliced
- 1 cup baked ham, cut in small pieces
- 12 oven-ready lasagna noodles
- 9 hard-boiled eggs, shelled and sliced
- 1/2 cup mozzarella cheese, grated

Preheat oven to 350°F. Lightly grease a 9-inch ×

13-inch baking pan. Mix the soup and the milk in a 4-cup glass measuring cup until well blended. In a medium-sized bowl, mix cottage (or ricotta) cheese, spinach, 3/4 cup of the soup mixture, 1/4 cup Parmesan, the scallions and ham. Spread 1/4 cup of the remaining soup mixture in the baking dish. Place 3 of the oven-ready lasagna noodles crosswise in the dish, not touching, and about 1/2 inch from the sides. Spread about 1 1/2 cups of the cheese mixture on the noodles. Top with 3 sliced eggs. Repeat twice. Top with the remaining 3 noodles, then pour on the rest of the soup mixture and sprinkle with the mozzarella cheese and the remaining Parmesan cheese. Cover dish tightly with foil. Bake 45 minutes, then uncover and bake another 10 to 15 minutes or until the top is golden brown. Remove from the oven, cover loosely and let stand about 10 minutes before cutting. Serves 6.

Sunday April 23

Easter Sunday

"Christ the Lord has risen today"
Sons of men and angels say.
Raise your joys and triumphs high;
Sing, ye heavens, and earth reply.

Charles Wesley

I wish all of the Christian faith a happy Easter!

Monday April 24

YOU have to count on living every single day in a way you believe will make you feel good about your life—so that if it were over tomorrow you'd be content with yourself.

Author unknown

Tuesday April 25

There's always a burst of sunshine
After a shower of rain;
There's always a time of happiness
After a spell of pain;
May the guardian angels watch you
With a vigil not in vain,
For the great outdoors is waiting
To welcome you again.

Author unknown

Wednesday April 26

THE leaves of the winter wither and sink in the forest mould to colour the flowers of April with purple and white and gold.

Alfred Noyes

Thursday April 27

MY son-in-law Bruce seems to spend his life fighting the "battle of the bulge." Although he eats carefully—doing his best to eat lots of fruits and vegetables, while restricting his fat intake—he seldom has time to exercise. You can imagine then, how excited he was to hear about an interesting theory that originated in England.

Researchers feel that you can build muscles, slim down and shape up just by thinking about it. Their theory is that if you visualize yourself exercising, you can achieve nearly half the benefit of a strenuous workout. The experts also theorize that mental exercise triggers changes in the body, just as physical exercise does.

When I last saw Bruce, he was sitting in his recliner chair and, according to him, running the Boston marathon.

Friday April 28

THE longer I live, the more I am convinced that the one thing worth living for and dying for is the privilege of making someone more happy and more useful. No man who ever does anything to lift his fellows ever makes a sacrifice.

Booker T. Washington

Saturday April 29

A DEAR friend brought me a beautiful bouquet of flowers that included many purple violets. Seeing these exquisite little flowers brought back an almost forgotten memory.

My mother used to make candied violet bouquets to decorate special cakes or jars of jelly that she gave to her close friends.

My sister, Sarah, and I would help by picking clean, long-stemmed purple violets, which we would lay on paper to dry. Mother would use an artist's brush that had been dipped into whipped egg whites to "paint" each flower and stem and, while they were still wet, she would dip the flowers into granulated sugar. Each flower was then placed on waxed paper to dry.

When the violets had dried thoroughly, Mother would put five or six of these flowers together and tie the bouquet with a bit of purple ribbon. These exquisite posies made a beautiful—and delicious—addition to any gift.

They also made a wonderful memory for me.

Sunday April 30

I AM the resurrection, and the life: he that believeth in me, though he were dead, yet shall he live: and whosoever liveth and believeth in me shall never die.

John 11:25–26

May

Monday May 1

Now the bright morning Star, Day's harbinger
Comes dancing from the East, and leads with
  her
The flowery May, who from her green lap
  throws
The yellow cowslip and pale primrose.
Hail bounteous May! Thou dost inspire
Mirth and youth and warm desire;
Woods and gloves are of the dressing;
Hill and dale dost boast thy blessing.
Thus we salute thee with our early song,
And welcome thee and wish thee long.

John Milton

Tuesday May 2

OUR life is like some vast lake that is slowly
filling with the stream of our years. As the
water creeps surely upward, the landmarks of the
past are one by one submerged. But there shall
always be memory to lift its head above the tide
until the lake is overflowing.

Alexander Bisson

Wednesday May 3

AS the baseball season gets underway, the fans will again take great pleasure in berating the umpires and questioning their every call. For many team followers, these attacks on the umpires' credibility is just another part of the game.

A big league umpire once remarked that he could never understand how crowds in the stands, hundreds of feet from home plate, could see better and judge balls and strikes more accurately than he, when he was only a few feet away.

All of us who are devotees of the game, whether or not we like the umpires' calls, look forward to those exciting words, "Play ball!"

Thursday May 4

PEOPLE who have warm friends are healthier and happier than those who have none. A single real friend is a treasure worth more than gold or precious stones. Money can buy many things, good and evil. All the wealth in the world could not buy you a friend, or pay you for the loss of one.

G. D. Prentice

Friday May 5

Count that day lost whose low descending sun
Views from thy hand no worthy action done.

Author unknown

As the sun sinks in the west and the evening shadows mark the end of the day, we need to pause and make note of what we have done to make this world a better place.

How many of us, looking back on the day that is past, can say truthfully that we have made the best of our opportunities; that we have done something worthwhile for the good of ourselves, our friends and our neighbours?

All of us have a part to play in the game of life but, as in all games, it is with teamwork that we succeed.

For our own part, we need to have a definite purpose in life and make plans to fulfill this purpose. By having a plan and trying to be successful with it, our retrospection at the end of the day becomes a source of satisfaction for something accomplished, for something given back to the world. And really, this is what life is all about, isn't it?

Saturday May 6

IF a man could mount to heaven and survey the mighty universe, his admiration of its beauties would be much diminished unless he had someone to share his pleasure.

Cicero

Sunday May 7

AT our church service this morning, we sang one of my favourite hymns. I hope it is one of yours too.

> For the beauty of the earth,
> For the glory of the skies,
> For the love which from our birth
> Over and around us lies,
> Lord of all to thee we raise
> This our grateful psalm of praise.

F. S. Pierpoint

Monday May 8

NATURE gives to every time and season some beauties of its own; and from morning to night, as from the cradle to the grave, is but a succession of changes so gentle and easy that we can scarcely mark their progress.

Charles Dickens

Tuesday May 9

BE not anxious about tomorrow. Do today's duty, fight today's temptation, and do not weaken and distract yourself by looking forward to things which you cannot see, and could not understand if you saw them.

Charles Kingsley

Wednesday May 10

ACCORDING to the experts, there is a frightening rise in the number of overweight children in North America. Here in Canada, it is estimated that more than a million children are too heavy. This statistic probably shouldn't surprise us. Television, computers and video games have become such a large part of children's daily lives that much less time is spent being physically active. Young people of today are eating the same number of calories (or even less than years ago) but, because the level of physical activity is lower, calories are not being burned off and children are gaining weight. Because 50 percent of overweight children are quite likely to become overweight adults, members of the medical community fear that the incidence of future health problems, such as heart disease, diabetes or arthritis, may increase dramatically.

Is there anything that parents can do to help prevent obesity? Experts suggest that when children are given a variety of healthy foods, including many fruits and vegetables, at an early age, they will choose a healthy diet for the rest of their lives.

Parents can also be role models. Those parents who are physically active are much more likely to have children who are too.

Schools should also be encouraged to offer strong physical education programs. Parents, teachers and the medical community can work together to ensure that we are bringing up a generation of fit and healthy young people.

Thursday May 11

EVERY man who knows how to read, has it in his power to magnify himself, to multiply the ways in which he exists, to make his life full, significant and interesting.

Aldous Huxley

Friday May 12

MARGARET and I went to visit a young neighbour at the Hospital for Sick Children, in Toronto. What a magnificent facility it is! Renowned worldwide, the hospital has the very best of equipment in a spectacularly beautiful building, and staff who are not only gifted in dealing with children but also upbeat, cheerful and fun loving.

As we moved through the hospital I was amazed by the preponderance of bright colours. Gone are the "hospital whites" or drab green of yesteryear. In their place are bright reds, greens, pinks, yellows and blues—on the walls or in the cheery fabric of the uniforms worn by the hospital staff.

Some of the uniforms may have come from a

company called S.C.R.U.B.S.—Simply Comfortable Really Unique Basic Scrubs—a company founded in California by a Canadian nurse, Sue Callaway. Needing something to boost her spirits, she began sewing her own scrubs, the usually dreary coloured cotton outfits worn by the workers in medical facilities. Co-workers loved her bright colours and asked Sue to make some uniforms for them. Her small cottage industry soon grew into an operation with 120 employees and is still growing. Along with a store in Santee, California, Sue has a monthly catalogue that introduces new fabrics and uniform designs.

Judging from the cheery uniforms worn by the staff at "Sick Kids," Sue Callaway will continue to be highly successful with her company.

Saturday May 13

WINSTON Churchill, shortly before his death, remarked, "I am ready to meet my Maker. Whether my Maker is ready for the great ordeal of meeting me is another matter."

Sunday May 14

Mother's Day

I SHALL never forget my mother, for it was she who planted and nurtured the first seeds of good within me. She opened my heart to the impressions of nature; she awakened my understanding and extended my horizon, and her precepts exerted an everlasting influence upon the course of my life.

Immanuel Kant

Monday May 15

IF you find that you cannot be with someone unless you're doing something together—skiing, going to a play, something to which you both direct your attention—then that person may not be as good a friend as you think.

The real test of friendship is: Can you literally do nothing with the other person? Can you enjoy together those moments of life that are utterly simple? They are the moments that people look back on at the end of life and number as their most cherished experiences.

E. Kennedy

Tuesday May 16

JAMES A. Michener, in his book *Space*, wrote: "Space is limitless. It goes on forever. Always remember that you and I live on a minor planet attached to a minor star, at the far edge of a minor galaxy. We live here briefly, and when we're gone, we're forgotten. And one day the galaxies will be gone too. The only morality that makes sense is to do something useful with the brief time we're allowed."

Wednesday May 17

THIS summer one-third of the nation will be ill housed, ill nourished and ill clad. Only they'll call it a vacation.

Thursday May 18

The old days, the far days,
The ever dear and fair,
The old days, the lost days—
How lovely they were!
The old days of morning,
With dew drench on the flowers
And apple buds and blossoms
As those old days of ours.

Then was the real gold
Spendthrift summer flung;
Then was the real song
Bird or poet sung!
There was never censure then,
Only honest praise,
And all things were worthy of it
In the old days.

There bide the true friends,
The first and the best;
There clings the green grass
Close where they rest.
Would they were here? No,
Would we were there!
The old days, the lost days—
How lovely they were!

James Whitcomb Riley

Friday May 19

HAPPINESS or unhappiness depends more on the way we meet events than on the nature of those events themselves.

Saturday May 20

AS is our family tradition, we are enjoying the long weekend here in Muskoka with my dear friend Eleanor. Since her husband Bob's passing, Marg, Bruce and I have spent this Victoria Day weekend helping Eleanor to open up her cottage. We have come to love this yearly ritual.

Many years ago the cottage opening was an event to be endured, certainly not enjoyed. But thanks now to modern conveniences such as vacuum cleaners, refrigerator-freezers, microwave ovens, electric water pumps, etc., the first yearly trip to the cottage is not much more work than a midsummer visit.

While Bruce removed the winter shutters, Marg and Eleanor shined the windows and I dusted and vacuumed each room and, in a matter of just a few hours, the place was ship-shape— ready for the summer fun. As we watched the sun sink, I was reminded of these lines.

Beauty seen is never lost
God's colours all are fast;
The glory of this sunset heaven
Into my soul has passed.

Alfred Lord Tennyson

Sunday May 21

Breathe on me, breath of God,
Fill me with life anew,
That I might love what thou dost love,
And do what thou wouldst do.

Breathe on me, breath of God,
So shall I never die,
But live with thee the perfect life
Of thine eternity.

Rev. Edwin Hatch

Monday May 22

SOME feel honoured when they are put at the table where the best linen and china are laid out. But the ones who are really honoured are those who are set at a table where the dishes don't match and the eating utensils are recruited from the kitchen. They are the true and trusted friends who do not need to be complimented or impressed and who would never think of criticizing.

And they are, therefore, the most honoured.

Author unknown

Those words came to mind as the four of us enjoyed our evening meal in the kitchen at Eleanor's cottage.

Our friendship is such that there is never a need for pretense. We are as comfortable in Eleanor's kitchen as we are in our own.

We are true and trusted friends and "the most honoured."

Tuesday May 23

THERE is an Indian belief that everyone is a house of four rooms; a physical, a mental, an emotional and a spiritual. Most of us tend to live in one room most of the time, but unless we go into every room everyday, even if it is only to keep it aired, we are not complete.

R. Godden

Wednesday May 24

ON this date in 1819, Princess Alexandria Victoria was born in London, England. She was the daughter of Prince Edward, Duke of Kent, and Princess Victoria, and was destined to become the longest reigning monarch in Britain's history.

Throughout the British Empire in the previous centuries, it was the custom to celebrate the birthday of the monarch with a holiday. Because Victoria's birthday was celebrated for such a long time, it was made a permanent holiday and, since 1952, it has been celebrated in Canada on the Monday preceding May 24.

Parades, concerts and a sailpast in the harbour are just some of the events held to honour this monarch of great moral strength and directness of character.

Thursday May 25

PARENTS of teens would make great tightrope artists—we've had so much practice. We are always walking that fine line between too far away and too close. We must never be snoopy, but always interested. We should blend with the scenery but stand firm as a rock when needed—which is oftener than we may think.

H. Bottel

Friday May 26

MY dear friend Lila, who is living in our local nursing home, gave me these lines from their monthly newsletter. I enjoyed them very much and I hope that you will too.

"Days were plentiful and cheap when I was young. Like penny candy, I always had a pocketful—and spent them casually. Now my supply is diminished and their value has soared. Each one becomes worth its weight in the gold of dawn. Suddenly I live in unaccustomed thrift, cherishing hours the way lovers prize moments. Even at that, when the week is ended, it seems I've gone through another fortune. A day doesn't go as far as it used to."

My thanks to the unknown author.

Saturday May 27

LOVE, and you shall be loved.

Sunday May 28

Rogation Sunday

ALMIGHTY and merciful God, from whom cometh every good and perfect gift; Bless, we beseech thee, the labours of thy people, and cause the earth to bring forth her fruits abundantly in their season, that we may with grateful hearts give thanks to thee for the same; Through Jesus Christ our Lord. Amen.

The Book of Common Prayer

Monday May 29

IF you have been to Ottawa during the month of May, you will have seen a spectacular sight on Parliament Hill. Hundreds of thousands of tulips bloom each spring, and they are a reminder of our special ties to Holland during the Second World War. At that time, Princess Julianna of the Netherlands lived in Ottawa, where her parents hoped to keep her safe from harm.

As well, the Canadian Armed Forces were a large part of the Allied group that was instrumental in the liberation of Holland. People were starving when the Canadians arrived, bringing food and freedom to the beleaguered Dutch.

As a token of appreciation, the Dutch sent four million tulip bulbs to Ottawa. Hundreds of thousands of these beautiful flowers continue to bloom each year and they are a magnificent sight.

Tuesday May 30

THE youth gets together his material to build a bridge to the moon, or, perchance a palace or temple on the earth, and, at length, the middle-aged man concludes to build a woodshed with them.

Henry David Thoreau

Wednesday May 31

ALBERT Schweitzer offered his philosophy of life.

"To know the will of God is the greatest knowledge.

To suffer the will of God is the greatest heroism.

To do the will of God is the greatest achievement.

To have the approval of God on your work is the greatest happiness."

June

Thursday June 1

THIS, the fortieth day after Easter, is Ascension Day. This is the day that Jesus ascended into heaven. This wonderful premise is the basis for our belief in eternal life. I think Phillips Brooks' words on immortality are most appropriate for today.

"The great Easter truth is not that we are to live newly after death—that is not the great thing—but that we are to be new here and now by the power of the resurrection; not so much that we may last forever as that we are to, and may, live nobly now because we are to live forever."

Friday June 2

YESTERDAY was the anniversary of my marriage, so many years ago. My husband, George, and I enjoyed a wonderful life together and his early passing was a difficult blow to accept. In his honour I offer these words by Henry Van Dyke.

Time is...
Too slow for those who wait,
Too swift for those who fear,
Too long for those who grieve,
Too short for those who rejoice;
But for those who love, time is an eternity.

Saturday June 3

MY good friends Will and Muriel stopped by today to bring me a bouquet of daffodils. Will is a "gardener extraordinaire," who frequently provides us with exquisite bouquets of flowers grown in his own garden. He also likes to help Marg, Bruce and I (all of whom seem to be "horticulturally challenged") to organize and plant a garden that will look quite lovely with a minimum of care.

Will and Muriel's garden is the envy of their neighbours and, as Muriel is quick to point out, "With no help from me."

Today, Will brought along a sheet of paper with several amusing definitions for "the beginning gardener." He seemed to think that we qualify.

Annual: any plant that dies before blooming.

Seed catalogues and garden brochures: entertaining fiction that is published by nurseries and garden tool manufacturers.

Furrow: horizontal line on the forehead of a gardener.

Perennial: any plant which, had it lived, would have bloomed year after year.

Seed: highly nutritious form of birdseed sold in attractive packets.

Sunday June 4

FEAR not, O land; be glad and rejoice: for the Lord will do great things.

Be not afraid, ye beasts of the field: for the pastures of the wilderness do spring, for the tree beareth her fruit, the fig tree and the vine do yield their strength.

Joel 2:21–22

Monday June 5

The Violet

Down in a green and shady bed
A modest violet grew,
Its stalk was bent; it hung its head,
As if to hide from view.

And yet it was a lovely flower,
Its colour bright and fair;
It might have graced a rosy bower,
Instead of hiding there.

Yet there it was, content to bloom,
Its modest tints arrayed;
And there diffused a sweet perfume,
Within the silent shade.

Then let me to the valley go,
This pretty flower to see,
That I may also learn how to grow
In sweet humility.

Jane Taylor

Tuesday June 6

Our lives are filled with simple joys
And blessings without end,
And one of the greatest joys in life
Is to have a friend.

Author unknown

Each year, as I grow older, I find that I treasure my friendships, and the joy that they bring to my life, more and more. It is comforting to be close to people who have done what I have done, seen what I have seen and lived through the same good times and bad. Old friends provide a comfort that is a treasure to the soul. As Henry Van Dyke said, "A friend is what the heart needs all the time."

Wednesday June 7

NOTHING in the world can take the place of persistence. Talent will not; nothing is more common than unsuccessful men with talent. Genius will not; unrewarded genius is almost a proverb. Education will not; the world is full of educational failures. Persistence and determination alone are omnipotent.

Calvin Coolidge

Thursday June 8

DISHONESTY is like a boomerang. About the time you think all is well, it hits you in the back of the head.

Friday June 9

HOW quickly my birthday seems to have come—again. Although I would like to forget the passing of the years, my friends and family seem doggedly determined to have me celebrate the day.

In keeping with a tradition established several years ago, my friends and family members have taken money, which they would have spent on a gift for me, and used it to do something nice for themselves. They then sent me a card to tell me how they used their "gift." How much I enjoy the cards!

My great-grandson, Mickey, who is at university, took a close friend out to a fine restaurant for dinner.

"John comes from a family of seven children, Gran, and there was never enough money for eating out. We had a wonderful meal and John thinks your idea of a birthday present is fantastic. Happy birthday and thank you, Gran!"

Marg chose to donate a book to the library, and Mary sent a contribution to the Cancer Society.

The twins, Justin and Jenny, went to a theatre production in Toronto, and their card described in wonderful detail how much they enjoyed the musical.

All in all, if one must have a birthday, this is a most satisfying way to celebrate.

Saturday June 10

WHAT a wee little part of a person's life are his acts and his words! His real life is led in his head, and is known to none but himself. All day long, the mill of his brain is grinding, and his thoughts, not those other things, are his history. These are his life and they are not written, and cannot be written. Every day would make a whole book of 80,000 words—365 books a year. Biographies are all but the clothes and buttons of the man—the biography of the man himself cannot be written.

Mark Twain

Sunday June 11

Whitsunday

GOD, who at this time didst teach the hearts of thy faithful people, by the sending to them the light of thy Holy Spirit; Grant us by the same Spirit to have a right judgement in all things, and evermore to rejoice in his holy comfort; through the merits of Christ Jesus our Saviour, who liveth and reigneth with thee, in the unity of the same Spirit, one God, world without end. Amen.

The Collect for the day of Pentecost

Monday June 12

I WONDER how many of my readers remember the first or second Sunday in June being known as Decoration Sunday (or Memorial Day). This was a tradition kept long before the days of commercial cemeteries or crematoriums. Then, the cemetery was kept either by a church or a small community. No endowments existed to pay for a cemetery caretaker. Instead, as soon as crops were sown and gardens planted, there would be a "cleaning bee" where families would work to clean and tidy up the cemetery, mowing the grass and planting flowering annuals on the gravesites of their forebears.

Then on the first or second Sunday in June (often depending upon the weather), there would be a memorial service in the cemetery with the village band playing and a guest clergy coming to preach.

The memorial service was usually followed by a special supper served in the basement of the church or perhaps at the home of a parishioner. It was a time to renew friendships and spend time in the fellowship of families and neighbours.

Although this tradition has become a memory in most areas, there are still small or remote communities across Canada that celebrate Decoration Day on the first two June weekends.

Tuesday June 13

WHEN you love someone you do not love them all the time, in exactly the same way, from moment to moment. It is an impossibility. It is even a lie to pretend to. And yet, this is exactly what most of us demand. We have so little faith in the ebb and flow of life, of love, of relationships. We leap at the flow of time and resist in terror its ebb. We are afraid it will never return. We insist on permanency, on duration, on continuity; when the only continuity possible, in life as in love, is growth, in fluidity—in freedom.

The only real security is not in owning or possessing, not in demanding or expecting, not in hoping, even. Security in a relationship lies neither in looking back to what it was, nor forward to what it might be, but living in the present and accepting it as it is now.

Ann Morrow Lindbergh

Wednesday June 14

WE are more easily persuaded, in general, by the reasons we ourselves discover than by those which are given to us by others.

Blaise Pascal

Thursday June 15

IN the middle of difficulty lies opportunity.

Albert Einstein

Friday June 16

And what is so rare as a day in June?
Then, if ever, comes perfect days;
The heaven tries earth, if it be in tune,
And over it softly her warm ear lays;
Whether we look, or whether we listen,
We hear life murmur, or see it glisten,
Every clod feels a stir of might,
An instinct within it that reaches and towers,
And grasping blindly above it for light,
Clings to a soul in grass and flowers.

James Russell Lowell

I am always happy when the month of June arrives because it heralds the coming of my favourite season, summer. The warmth, sometimes overpowering when I was younger, is now such a comfort for my old bones. Age does have its own rewards.

Saturday June 17

IT is an interesting fact that sheep sometimes get lost by nibbling away at grass and never looking up. We would do well to remember this premise ourselves. Sometimes we focus so intently on immediate tasks or problems that we fail to see the whole picture. We would be wise to remember that we need to take our eyes from "the grass" and see our life in larger perspective.

Sunday June 18

A Father's Prayer

Lord teach me understanding
That I may know the way to my child's heart
   and mind;
Give me strength,
That I may not fail him in minor tragedies or in
   great crises;
Give me courage,
That I may stand firm when he is wrong, or

> wayward or heedless;
> Grant me humility,
> That I may acknowledge my own mistake
> when he is right.

I have so many wonderful memories of my father. He was a man of principle and honour. He set high standards and lived his life by them. What a fine example he set for us children, and how well he brought us to adulthood with his unending love.

Monday June 19

TO be content, just think how happy you would be if you lost everything you have right now...and then got it back.

Tuesday June 20

A ROOM without books is like a man without a soul.

Cicero

Wednesday June 21

SUMMER afternoon—summer afternoon, to me those have always been the two most beautiful words in the English language.

Henry James

Today I welcome summer, my favourite season of the year. Today is the longest day of the year, with the most daylight hours to enjoy. In Canada, the farther north you go, the more daylight hours there are. In the far north, where the sun never sets on this day, some people hold a "Summer Solstice Party." Entire communities will celebrate with picnics, potluck dinners and all-night dances. I like to think of it as a special reward for northerners, helping to compensate for the winter solstice in December, when the sun never rises.

We will delight in time spent in our garden and look forward to the many joys that the summer season brings.

Thursday June 22

THERE are two things to aim at in life: first to get what you want; and after that, to enjoy it. Only the wisest of mankind achieve the second.

Logan Piersall

Friday June 23

THE ornaments of a home are the friends that frequent it.

Ralph Waldo Emerson

Saturday June 24

Past Junes have a way of coming back, disguised
Ingeniously. A fragile-petaled rose
Transports me to a porch where dusk surprised
The rocking chairs. A wide winged night
    moth goes
Up the gray trellis. Mother lifts her shawl,
A ghost thing, from the railing, nestles it
About her throat against the first damp.
    Words fall
Into the yard where firefly lamps are lit,
Melt into silence and are gently gone.

Then, as the breeze walks leaf trails overhead,
The dog moves shadowed on the cool soft lawn,
Father sends pipe smoke toward the lily bed
And dark treads purposefully down the street,
Sure that its welcome will be soft and sweet.

Marie Daerr

Sunday June 25

O THAT men would praise the Lord for his goodness, and for his wonderful works to the children of men! For he satisfieth the longing soul, and filleth the hungry soul with goodness.

Psalm 107:8–9

Monday June 26

THIS past weekend the province of Québec celebrated *Fête nationale*, also known as St. Jean Baptiste Day.

In many of the smaller towns and villages, this is a day of family get-togethers, and many groups enjoy fireworks as part of the evening celebrations. In larger cities, there are parades, and in Montréal, Mass is celebrated on the square in front of Notre Dame Cathedral.

It is a time to celebrate, with pride, the unique heritage that is our French Canadian province.

Tuesday June 27

WHEN a friend is in trouble, don't annoy him by asking if there is something you can do. Think of something appropriate and just do it!

Wednesday June 28

NOTHING is more pleasant than greenery washed by a rain and dried by the sun into cleanliness and warmth. Gardens and meadows, with moisture at their roots and sunshine on their blossoms, become jars of incense, each giving out its scent. The world smiles and bestows itself, and we feel a gentle intoxication. The sun teaches men to endure.

Victor Hugo

Thursday June 29

ONE of the most delicious treats that the month of June brings is red and juicy strawberries. There are probably hundreds of ways to enjoy the delectable fruit. One of my favourites is a tempting dessert called Strawberry Delight.

1 cup flour
1/4 cup brown sugar
1/2 cup pecans, chopped
1/2 cup butter (or margarine), melted
1 1/2 cups fresh strawberries
1 cup white sugar
2 tsp. fresh lemon juice
2 egg whites
1/2 pint whipping cream

Preheat oven to 350°F. Combine flour, brown sugar, pecans, and butter. Put in a 9-inch square baking pan. Bake 20 minutes, stirring often. Remove from oven and let cool. In a blender, combine strawberries, white sugar, lemon juice and egg whites. Blend at high speed until fluffy. (This may take up to 20 minutes.) Fold in whipping cream. Remove about 1/3 of the pecan mixture and set aside. Pat the remaining pecan mixture into a smooth layer in the baking pan. Pour the strawberry mixture over the pecan mixture in the pan and sprinkle the remaining pecan mixture over the top. Freeze. To serve, cut into squares and garnish with whole fresh strawberries.

Friday June 30

WHEN one reaches my advanced years, people begin to ask if there is some secret to longevity. I always answer that it is "good health and good luck."

There are a few things that I believe have helped me, but I certainly don't claim to be any kind of expert. Along with the most obvious—good diet, regular exercise and regular medical checkups—I try to keep a positive attitude, and I do my best to keep mentally active. I read the newspapers, do crossword puzzles, visit the library frequently and try to do mental puzzles to keep my faculties functioning.

I also enjoy daily contact with friends and family. As we age, and our friends pass away, it is important that we not become isolated. Church groups or social clubs can provide a place to laugh and share our joys and sorrows.

It is also important for me to take each day as it comes and enjoy it to the fullest measure.

July

Saturday July 1
Canada Day

IN whichever province or territory you live, today is the day to celebrate the unity of our country "from sea to sea." Picnics, parades and firework displays are the most common ways to commemorate the day, but there are hundreds of uncommon ways to celebrate as well. Giant birthday cakes, sidewalk art, horseshoe competitions, gopher races or lighted boat parades are just a few of the ways that we Canadians, old and new, choose to recognize our wonderful country.

An integral part of our celebration will be the singing of the national anthem, composed by Justice R.S. Weir in 1908. When sung with unbridled enthusiasm, there is for me no lovelier anthem in all the world.

O Canada! Our home and native land!
True patriot love, in all thy sons' command,
With glowing hearts, we see thee rise,
The true north strong and free!
From far and wide, O Canada,
We stand on guard for thee.

God keep our land, glorious and free,
O Canada, we stand on guard for thee,
O Canada, we stand on guard for thee!

Sunday July 2

O HEAVENLY Father, in whom we live and move and have our being: We humbly pray thee so to guide and govern us by thy Holy Spirit, that in all the cares and occupations of our daily life we may never forget thee, but remember that we are ever walking in thy sight; through Jesus Christ our Lord. Amen.

The Book of Common Prayer

Monday July 3

I TOOK my friend Lila for a long walk today. Lila has used a wheelchair for several years now, but she still enjoys being outdoors and seeing the old neighbourhood where she lived for many years. I love the exercise of pushing a wheelchair and the interesting turns that our conversations frequently take during these promenades. Lila is such a wise woman, and I feel that I learn something from her each time we visit.

I believe that Seneca could have been speaking of Lila when he said, "As for old age, embrace it and love it. It abounds with pleasure, if you know how to use it. The gradually (and I do not say rapidly) declining years are among the sweetest in a man's life; and I maintain that even where they have reached the extreme limit, they have their pleasure still."

Tuesday July 4

OUR American friends will celebrate "The Glorious Fourth" today. You would be hardpressed to find a more boisterously patriotic people in the world than the Americans, and on the fourth of July this enthusiasm knows no bounds.

Daniel Webster wrote, "Let our object be our country, our whole country and nothing but our country. And, by the blessing of God, may that country itself become a vast and splendid monument, not of oppression and terror, but of wisdom, of peace, and of liberty, upon which the world may gaze with admiration forever."

Wednesday July 5

HAN Suyin, author, made this wise observation: "I can't understand people who say, 'I've got two hours to kill.' I don't know the meaning of that expression 'to kill time.' What does it mean? Life is a gift. You should live every minute of it. When I hear things like that, I think the time will come when you will say, 'Give me two more hours to live!'"

Thursday July 6

KIND words can be short and easy to speak, but their echoes are truly endless.

Mother Teresa

Friday July 7

The little cares that fretted me,
I lost them yesterday
Among the fields above the sea,
Among the winds that play,
Among the lowing of the herds,
The rustling of the trees,
Among the singing of the birds,
The humming of the bees.

The foolish fears of what might pass,
I cast them all away
Among the clover-scented grass,
Among the new-mown hay,
Among the hushing of the corn,
Where drowsy poppies nod,
Where ill thoughts die and good are born—
Out in the fields of God.

Author unknown

Saturday July 8

ALL truly wise thoughts have been thought already thousands of times; but to make them really ours, we must think them over again honestly, till they take firm root in our personal experience.

Goethe

Sunday July 9

BLESSED be God, who hath not turned away my prayer, nor his mercy from me.

Psalm 66:20

Monday July 10

MANY years ago, my brother, Ben, and I were walking together through a field when we came upon a butterfly struggling to free itself from its cocoon. Ben, in an effort to be helpful, took out his small pocketknife and cut open the shell to free the butterfly. We sat watching and waiting for this beautiful insect to take flight, but it just lay there on the ground.

Not knowing what else to do, Ben placed the butterfly on his hand and carried it home to show our father.

Father explained that this butterfly would be forever earthbound. "You see, Ben," he said, "it is in the struggle to free itself that the wings develop and strengthen themselves. Without the hard work, the wings will never be strong enough to fly."

We would be wise to remember this simple illustration in our own lives. Often we look for shortcuts to fulfill some ambition or dream, when what we really need to do is to struggle, and continue to work hard.

As someone once said, "Nothing worthwhile was ever accomplished without hard work."

Tuesday July 11

MANY people are like blisters—they don't show up until the work is all done!

Wednesday July 12

MARCUS Tullius Cicero wrote in praise of literature: "But this gives stimulus to our youth and diversion to our old age; this adds charm to success, and offers a haven of consolation to failure. In the home it delights, in the world it hampers not. Through the night watches, on all our journeying, and in our hours of country ease, it is an unfailing companion."

Thursday July 13

MY friend Marcia, who lives in Boston, has a sense of humour that greatly appeals to me. She wrote to me this week: "My favourite expression used to be 'A place for everything and everything in its place.' Well, I do have a place for everything, only I keep changing the place. Of course I lose a lot of time looking for things and wondering where I put them. But it's such a thrill when my mind begins to function, and I remember the newest place.

"It's even more fun when suddenly I spot something by sheer accident after I had about given up hope of ever finding it—like my emerald ring, which I found in the meat compartment of the refrigerator. And who said growing old isn't exciting?"

Friday July 14

I AM grown peaceful as old age tonight, I regret a little, I would change still less.

Robert Browning

Saturday July 15

MY son-in-law Bruce and my grandson Marshall thoroughly enjoy their Saturday morning golf games together. Both have played long enough to become quite proficient, so now they are able to play a round without having to spend inordinate amounts of time searching for lost balls or, on occasion, lost clubs.

I like to hear the inevitable golf jokes that are also a part of the Saturday ritual between father and son.

A foursome was playing on a course where the road ran parallel to the third hole. A limousine pulled up alongside the group as they walked along the fairway. It stopped and a beautiful girl in a wedding dress jumped out, threw her arms around one of the golfers and cried, "John! John! Why have you left me waiting at the altar?"

"Now, now, Claire," he said sternly. "Remember—I said *if it rained*."

Sunday July 16

Now the day is over,
Night is drawing nigh,
Shadows of the evening
Steal across the sky.

Now the darkness gathers,
Stars their watches keep,
Birds and beasts and flowers
Soon will be asleep.

Jesu give the weary
Calm and sweet repose;
With thy tenderest blessing
May mine eyelids close.

Rev. S. Baring-Gould

Monday July 17

AS the baseball season rolls along, I follow with great interest the fate of "my boys," the Toronto Blue Jays. Knowing of my relatively new interest in the game, my friend Jake Frampton likes to pass along interesting but little-known facts about various players in years past.

I found it very interesting to learn that in 1932, when the New York Yankees traded away their aging superstar Babe Ruth, it was a Canadian who took his place in the outfield. George Selkirk, of Huntsville, Ontario, nicknamed "Twinkletoes," was assigned the beloved Bambino's position and uniform number.

Tuesday July 18

MY daughter Julia recently returned from a trip to our nation's capital, Ottawa. While there, she took a trip on the Rideau Canal, the historic waterway linking Ottawa to the St. Lawrence River.

Used now for pleasure boating, the canal was originally built after the War of 1812 with the Americans. Wary of the fact that the St. Lawrence River, our major transportation corridor, lay close to the U. S. border (indeed, in parts it actually forms the border), the Duke of Wellington commissioned Colonel John By to build the canal that would link Ottawa to

Kingston, well away from possible American military action.

It took the 2,000 men five years to hack through bush, dig trenches and haul the enormous limestone blocks that would build the 50 dams and 47 locks that make up the Rideau Canal. Opened in 1832, the 200-kilometre-long canal today remains exactly as it was then, right down to the hand operation of its locks and swing bridges.

Designated by the federal government as an historical monument, the canal is now operated by Parks Canada. It is an enduring—and durable—legacy of a bygone era.

Wednesday July 19

Yellow butterflies
  Over the blooming virgin corn
With pollen-painted faces
  Chase one another in the brilliant throng.

Hopi Song

Thursday July 20

WE should be careful to get out of an experience only the wisdom that is in it—and stop there; lest we be like the cat that sits down on a hot stove-lid. She will never sit down on a hot stove-lid again—and that is well; but also, she will never sit down on a cold one anymore.

Mark Twain

Friday July 21

BRANCH Rickey, a former baseball commissioner, made this observation. He could be speaking for almost any father.

"The most important single qualification a man should have to marry one of my daughters is infinite kindness. Infinite kindness will sustain a marriage through all of its problems, its uncertainties, its illnesses, its disappointments, its storms, its tensions, its fears, its separations, its fears, its sorrows. Out of infinite kindness grows real love and understanding, tolerance and warmth.

"Nothing can take the place of such an enduring asset."

Saturday July 22

THE long lazy days of summer have arrived and with them come some of the simple pleasures that are strictly for the summer. This is my list—you may add your own ideas to it:

A frosty cold glass of lemonade,
The murmur of wind chimes,
The breeze as it blows across the porch,

Queen Anne's lace,
The cry of the loon,
The taste of a ripe tomato,
A swim in a cool lake,
The smell of a newly mown lawn,
Fireflies flickering in the night,
Home-made ice cream,
Roses in the gardens,
Fresh raspberry pie,
Paddling in a canoe,
The night sounds of frogs and crickets and
    katydids,
Daisy chains.

Sunday July 23

THE 23rd Psalm is the nightingale of the psalms. It is small, of a homely feather, singing shyly out of obscurity; but, oh, it has filled the air of the whole world with melodious joy, greater than the heart can conceive. Blessed be the day on which that psalm was born.

Henry Ward Beecher

Monday July 24

BRUCE and Marg have some good friends who travel extensively. They have been to many exotic locations and met a wonderful variety of people from all walks of life. Bruce and

Marg enjoy their friends' trips vicariously through the postcards that they receive.

A California author, George Mair, has some rather unusual suggestions for postcard writing, guaranteed to pique the interest of the recipients back home.

He suggests that the postcard should be scrawled hastily in felt tipped pen, written diagonally; it should be legible but not excessively neat. The foreign stamp should be pasted on slightly askew.

Here are some sample messages.

"Hello, must hurry. They're coming over the wall."

"Can't imagine where we are going at this hour."

"Did you know that the Dalai Lama (or prince, or sheik, or cardinal) speaks Spanish?"

"It was the most grotesque (or breathtaking) thing we have ever seen. More later..."

And then this, the *pièce de résistance*:

"If you get this, there is a chance we made it out alive!"

Tuesday July 25

NEVER bear more than one kind of trouble at a time. Some people bear three—all they have had, all they have now and all they expect to have.

Edward Everett Hale

Wednesday July 26

WE'VE probably all heard, at one time or another, different rhymes about the weather. In years past, these rhymes were considered an important part of weather prediction. How many do you still rely upon?

A sunny shower
Won't last half an hour.

Rain before seven,
Fair by eleven.

Red sky at night is the sailor's delight;
Red sky at morning, sailors take warning.

If bees stay at home,
Rain will come soon,
If they fly away,
Fine will be the day.

When clouds appear like rocks and towers,
The earth's refreshed by frequent showers.

Thursday July 27

IS there anything more delicious than potato salad at a summer picnic? Almost every family has its own special recipe and we are no exception. This recipe comes from Jamie, my grandson Marshall's wife.

Picnic Potato Salad

4 – 5 cups cooked potatoes, diced
4 hard boiled eggs, chopped
1 medium onion, chopped
1/2 cup celery, chopped
1/2 cup radishes, sliced
Dressing:
    3/4 cup mayonnaise
    2/3 tbsp. mustard
    2 tbsp. vinegar
    1 tsp. sugar
    1/4 cup sweet pickle relish
    salt & pepper to taste

Combine all ingredients and refrigerate, preferably overnight. Serves 6.

Friday July 28

WE are all of us passengers on the same planet and we are all of us equally responsible for the happiness and the well-being of the world in which we happen to live.

Hendrik William Van Loon

Saturday July 29

IT is said that God gave us memory so we could have roses in winter. But it is also true that without memory we would not have a self in any season. The more memories you have, the more "you" you have.

George Will

Sunday July 30

HOW excellent is thy lovingkindness, O God! Therefore the children of men put their trust under the shadow of thy wings.

Psalm 36:7

Monday July 31

DURING the warm summer days and evenings, many campers and cottagers delight in using the canoe as a form of transportation or relaxation. It's interesting to note that, in spite of technological advances, no one has been able to improve upon the design of the Indian canoe. The birchbark may be replaced with canvas or fibreglass, but the lines and model are just the same.

August

Tuesday August 1

FOR centuries, people have fixed their eyes upon the heavens and dreamed, and poets have penned many an immortal line about stars. As Marg, Bruce and I sat stargazing in the garden this evening, I was reminded of these lines from Lord Byron.

> Ye stars! Which are the poetry of heaven,
> If in your bright leaves we could read the fate
> Of men and empires—'tis to be forgiven
> That in our aspirations to be great
> Our destinies o'erlap their mortal state
> And claim a kindred with you; for ye are
> A beauty and a mystery, and create
> In us such love and reverence from afar,
> That fortune, fame, power, life, have named
> Themselves a star.

Wednesday August 2

MARG received a bee sting this afternoon and we both reached for our favourite remedy at the same time—baking soda. I helped Marg make a paste with the soda and a little water, and we spread the paste over the affected area. Marg found it very soothing.

We use baking soda for so many things that Bruce refers to it as a miracle worker. Here are just a few of the ways that baking soda may be helpful to you.

A large can or jar full of baking soda may be used in the kitchen as a fire extinguisher for grease or fat fires. Toss the soda on the fire immediately.

Half a teaspoon of baking soda mixed in half a glass of water may be taken for emergency relief of acid indigestion.

Bruce occasionally uses three tablespoons of baking soda mixed in a small basin of warm water to replace shaving cream. It is particularly soothing for sensitive skin.

About one cup of baking soda added to a tub of warm water can be very soothing for sunburn or minor skin irritations.

Need to whiten your teeth? Baking soda, used as toothpaste, is an inexpensive whitener.

Thursday August 3

YOU can do anything if you have enthusiasm. Enthusiasm is the yeast that makes your hopes rise to the stars. Enthusiasm is the sparkle in your eyes, the swing in your gait, the grip of your hand, the irresistible surge of will and energy to execute your ideas.

Enthusiasts are fighters. They have fortitude. They have staying qualities. Enthusiasm is at the bottom of all progress. With it, there is only accomplishment. Without it, there are only alibis.

Henry Ford

Friday August 4

MY daughter Mary read these lines some years ago, and they seem to describe August to perfection.

"Why do they call them dog days? These are obviously cat days. When the soft August breeze is just right it seems to rub up against you with a purr. The late-gleaming sun, as the days get shorter, is golden as a cat's eye. And then the elements can start spitting and yowling when you least expect it; and humidity returns and you feel as though a Manx were sleeping on your chest.

"Like the smile of the Cheshire, cat days come and go. Dog days just lie there waiting for you to take the initiative."

Author unknown

Saturday August 5

I AM back in Muskoka for my annual visit with my dear friend Eleanor. How I love this beautiful area of Ontario! No matter how many times

I come here, I never tire of the rocks, trees and spectacular lakes that make the region beloved by thousands of cottagers.

This afternoon Eleanor and I, along with two other friends, took a boat cruise up into Lake Rosseau to visit one of the grand old hotels, Windermere House. In fact, Windermere cannot be called "old" as it has been rebuilt from the ashes of a devastating fire that burned the original building to the ground several years ago. Happily, this lovely hotel is almost an exact replica of the original hotel that welcomed summer visitors at the turn of the century. From the beautiful stone base to the wide porch with the welcoming wicker furniture, from the magnificent dining room to the red-roofed turrets, Windermere House is a look back at a bygone era—with all of today's luxuries.

We enjoyed a delicious lunch before embarking on our leisurely cruise back through the locks at Port Carling and down into Lake Muskoka. It was evening when we arrived at the cottage.

The day is done, the sun has set,
The light still tints the sky;
My heart stands still in reverence,
For God is passing by.

Ruth Alla Wager

Sunday August 6

All things bright and beautiful
All creatures great and small,
All things wise and wonderful
The Lord God made them all.

How appropriate that we sang this well-known hymn at church this morning. Here in Muskoka where we see so much of God's beautiful work, this hymn written by Cecil Francis Alexander seemed to be describing what was all around us in the little chapel.

He gave us eyes to see them,
And lips that we might tell
How great is God Almighty
Who has made all things well.

Monday August 7

THE first Monday in August is a holiday for most of us in Canada. It is generally known as the "Civic Holiday" and is celebrated in all provinces except Quebec. While it is a holiday of no particular religious or historical significance, the day has been uniquely named to suit each province.

In Nova Scotia, the day is called "Natal Day" in celebration of the founding of Halifax in 1749.

Ontario honours its first lieutenant governor, John Graves Simcoe, by naming today "Simcoe Day." Alberta and Saskatchewan celebrate "Heritage Day." In British Columbia, merrymakers enjoy "B.C. Day." Wherever you are, it is a day to enjoy our all-too-short summer weather.

Tuesday August 8

I ENJOYED this story that Eleanor told me today.

Several years ago, a 62-year-old gentleman, a worker at a gas-cooker factory in England, decided to put in for early retirement. His friends always told him that he looked very young for his age, but he was feeling a little sluggish and felt that retirement would be in his best interest. When the company wrote to the officials in Dublin for his birth certificate, they discovered that he was not 62—but 79 years old!

Wednesday August 9

The boundaries of heaven may be
Less wide than night's immensity,
Less high than snowy peaks or spires.
A lamplit pane, a kindled fire,
A room, an acre, or a mile,
Or the brief space it takes a smile

To cross the threshold of the heart—
These no cartographer may chart,
Or instrument have power to give
The latitude by which we live.

Rachel Field

Thursday August 10

EVENINGS at the cottage are often spent playing games. If there are four of us, we frequently indulge in a game of bridge. Other card games such as "hearts" or "spit" are also popular. Scrabble is another favourite game, although Eleanor is undisputed champion of that game, and the rest of us work to place second.

Our all-time favourite choice of games for the cottage, though, has to be Monopoly. There is a most interesting story of how this game came to be.

Out of work in Philadelphia during the Depression, Charles Darrow supported his family by fixing appliances, patching concrete and walking dogs. He also invented things—puzzles, beach toys, simple games and a bridge score pad.

In 1931 Darrow, who used to vacation in Atlantic City, sketched the names of various streets on a piece of oilcloth, coloured the spaces and cut out "houses" and "hotels" from bits of wood. He typed out title deeds and added dice and buttons for play money.

The family played night after night, and soon

friends wanted their own sets. Darrow obliged, selling the games for $2.50. At first he made six sets a day, but when Philadelphia stores needed more than he could produce, he sold his rights to Parker Brothers, and lived as a millionaire off the royalties. It remains one of the most popular games ever sold.

Friday August 11

High noon in August! Over all the land
The very air is palpitant with heat;
While stretching far, the fields of ripening wheat
Unrippled lie as plains of yellow sand!

Henry S. Cornwell

Saturday August 12

I HAVE three precious things which I hold fast and prize. The first is gentleness; the second is frugality; and the third is humility which keeps me from putting myself before others. Be gentle and you can be bold; be frugal and you can be liberal; avoid putting yourself before others, and you can become a leader among men.

Lao-tse, Chinese philosopher

Sunday August 13

THE Lord God Almighty grant us a quiet night, and at the last a perfect end; and the blessing of God Almighty, the Father, and Son, and the Holy Ghost, be with us this night, and for evermore. Amen.

The Book of Common Prayer

Monday August 14

AS Eleanor and I are both grandmothers and great-grandmothers, our discussions frequently centre on our families. One thing on which we both agree is our love of being a grandparent. Today, I offer a few thoughts on being this source of comfort, strength, tradition and history.

No matter what you do, your grandmother thinks it's wonderful.

Judith Levy

A grandmother will accept your calls from anywhere—collect.

Erma Bombeck

Grandmothers are always kind.

Louisa May Alcott

If nothing is going well, call your grandmother.

Italian proverb

The joy of becoming a mother was a prelude to the joy of becoming a grandmother.

Vera Allen-Smith

Grandmothers are voices of the past and role models of the present. Grandmothers open doors to the future.

Helen Ketchum

Tuesday August 15

OH the blessing it is to have a friend to whom we can speak fearlessly on any subject: one with whom deepest as well as one's most foolish thoughts come out simply and safely. Oh, the comfort, the inexpressible comfort of feeling safe with a person, having neither to weigh thoughts nor measure words, but pouring them all right out just as they come, chaff and grain together, certain that a faithful hand will take and sift them, keep what is worth keeping and then, with a breath of kindness, blow away the rest.

George Eliot

I feel so fortunate to have such a friend in Eleanor. If you too have such a friend, value them! They are a rare treasure.

Wednesday August 16

SCIENCE cannot solve the ultimate mystery of nature. And that is because, in the last analysis, we ourselves are part of nature, and therefore part of the mystery that we are trying to solve.

Max Planck

Thursday August 17

SEE everything, overlook a great deal, correct a little.

Pope John Paul XXIII

Friday August 18

THERE are many American families who choose to spend their summers here in Muskoka. This afternoon I had a chance to meet one of these young families and enjoy hearing stories of their days here in cottage country.

Annie and Johnnie Larkin and their three beautiful children, Sophie, Mary and Jack, come to Muskoka from San Antonio, Texas. In fact, Annie has been spending summers here since she was a child herself.

I had a good laugh this afternoon over this story of Annie's.

For a number of years now, the Larkins have had a Canadian nanny to care for their children here in the summer. Several years ago, Mary, who was only three at the time, began to pick up on her nanny Jamie's many Canadian expressions. One such phrase was "pardon me" which Jamie used frequently after a cough or hiccup or quiet burp. Mary grew quite fond of this expression and could often be heard saying in her cute Texan twang, "Oh, pahdon me."

The only problem was that Mary couldn't seem to find ways to use the expression often enough to suit her. And so began several weeks when this adorable little, blond, curly-haired child would swallow enough air to come out with an earth shaking "BUURRP!" and a delightful little "Oh, pahdon me" that would send the adults into fits of laughter—and her mother into red-faced embarrassment.

Saturday August 19

I KNOW I am somebody's friend if I think, "Oh isn't it wonderful that such a thing should be happening to so-and so," and feel happy for him or her. Sharing and experiencing other people's joy is what friendship is all about. Commiserating with their misfortune is not enough. Any kind of person would do that.

Carlo Maria Giulini

Sunday August 20

THEY that wait upon the Lord shall renew their strength; they shall mount up with wings as eagles; they shall run, and not be weary; and they shall walk, and not faint.

Isaiah 40:31

Monday August 21

THE heavens and the earth alike speak of God, and the great natural world is but another Bible, which clasps and binds the written one; for nature and grace are one—grace the heart of the flower, and nature in its surrounding petals.

Henry Ward Beecher

Tuesday August 22

LOVELY as it is to be with friends on holiday, it is lovelier still to return to home and family. Time away is often a reminder of how much our family means to us. Today I offer some wise words on home and family.

Family ties so gently teach you
How to give and how to care...
And family ties so warmly
Reach you anytime and anywhere.

Margaret Fishback

The home is the centre and circumference, the start and finish of most of our lives.

C. P. Gilman

In a world of constant change, we welcome the constant love of family.

Margaret Fishback

Home is the one place in all this world where hearts are sure of each other.

Frederick Robertson

No place is more delightful than one's own fireside.

Cicero

Every family has its own history, its own heart-beat...a family is where life begins and love happens.

Margaret Fishback

Wednesday August 23

PEOPLE who are always trying to get even, can hardly expect to get ahead.

Richard Armour

Thursday August 24

IN order to maintain a well-balanced perspective, the person who has a dog to worship him should also have a cat to ignore him.

Author unknown

Friday August 25

Be like the bird, halting in his flight
Awhile in boughs so light,
Feels them give way beneath him and yet sings
Knowing that he has wings.

Victor Hugo

Saturday August 26

THE life of every man is a diary in which he means to write one story, and writes another; and his humblest hour is when he compares the volume as it is with what he vowed to make it.

Author unknown

Sunday August 27

This is the day the Lord hath made
He calls the hours his own,
Let heavens rejoice, let earth be glad
And praise surround the throne.

Today he rose and left the dead
And Satan's empire fell;
Today the saints his triumph spread
And all his wonders tell.

Isaac Watts

Monday August 28

I ENJOY these lines from Goethe.

For A Contented Life

Health enough to make work a pleasure,
Wealth enough to support your needs,
Strength to battle with difficulties and over
    come them,
Grace enough to confess your sins and
    forsake them,
Patience enough to toil until some good is
    accomplished,
Charity enough to see some good in your
    neighbour,
Love enough to move you to be useful and
    helpful to others,
Faith enough to make real the things of God,
Hope enough to remove all anxious fears
    concerning the future.

Thursday August 29

IF I had my life to live over again, I would have made a rule to read some poetry and listen to some music at least once a week; for perhaps the parts of my brain now atrophied would thus have kept active through use.

The loss of these tastes is a loss of happiness, and may possibly be injurious to the intellect, and more probably the moral character, by enfeebling the emotional part of our nature.

Charles Darwin

Wednesday August 30

AS we advance in life, we acquire a keener sense of the value of time. Nothing else, indeed, seems of any consequence; and we become misers in this respect.

William Hazlitt

Thursday August 31

THE evenings are cooler now—a portent of the autumn to come. Some trees have a hint of the red and yellow leaves of fall, and the sun sets earlier each day. While I shall miss the warm days of summer, I look forward to the beauty of the autumn.

Autumn is a gypsy
With jewels in her hair.

From "A Gypsy Named Autumn" by
Isla Paschal Richardson

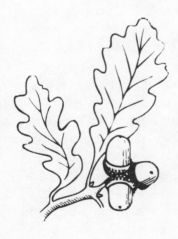

September

Friday September 1

I WATCHED a flock of geese fly overhead today, a sure sign that the fall season is close at hand. Seeing the geese brought to mind the words of Grace Noll Crowell's "Autumn Flight."

Now the wild geese are going over,
Clanking their chains on the windless sky,
Over the cornfields, over the clover,
Shouting their wild exuberant cry:
"Come with us, come with us—come."

They are calling,
And I, with no answer shaped in my mouth,
Stand where the painted leaves are falling,
Watching them disappear in the south,

Disappear from my sight and hearing,
Going to who knows what land,
Straight as an arrow, and not fearing
The journey ahead...

I lift my hand,
Bidding them stay their avid going
Across the wide uncharted track,
Calling to them, and yet well knowing
That only spring will bring them back.

Saturday September 2

THIS is the last long weekend of the summer season. While some people will choose to enjoy their cottages to the very last moment on Monday, others, often parents of school children, will be doing last-minute shopping for new outfits for their children to wear on the first day of school.

I must say that I don't envy parents who are attempting to dress their children while sticking to an expenditure that is anything less than the budget for a small country. I went shopping with Jamie as she searched for some school clothing for my great-granddaughter, Bethany, and I found the price of children's clothing to be flabbergasting. I realize that costs for everything have risen dramatically over the years, but I believe that George and I purchased a refrigerator and a stove for what it now costs to buy a small dress, socks, and a pair of shoes.

I guess that my age is showing!

Sunday September 3

ALMIGHTY God, your son Jesus Christ dignified our labour by sharing our toil. Be with your people wherever we work. Make those who carry on the industries and commerce of this land responsive to your will, and to all of us give pride in what we do and a just return for our labour, through your son Jesus Christ. Amen.

Author unknown

Monday September 4

Labour Day

TODAY is Labour Day, our final holiday of the summer. First celebrated by the Knights of Labour in New York City in 1882, and again in 1884, it is now a legal holiday in both the United States and Canada.

When I think of the word "labour," I like to remember people who are happy in their jobs. I think of the checkout girl who is never without a smile for her customers. I think of the school teacher who gives so freely of her time, coaching teams of boys and girls before and after school hours. I think of the pharmacist who brought my medication to me at home, when I couldn't get to the store on my own. Most of all, I remember my husband, George, who loved every minute of his "labour" in God's service.

Tuesday September 5

IN our area this is the first day of school. Watching the youngsters head off to the halls of learning, I thought of my own school days so very long ago, and these lines came to mind.

It was in the old frame schoolhouse
Our copy books we scanned...
We wrote on smooth clean pages
In blotless carefree hand.
These gems of thought we treasured
From childhood's carefree way...
Somehow we can't help feeling
They're just as true today.

Anne Campbell

Wednesday September 6

MOST teachers have their own unique ways of getting to know their students in the first few days of school. One of Jenny's teachers asks her students to complete a number of sentences, many of which are quite thought provoking. I think that the students may learn something about themselves as well. Here are some examples of the sentences that the students complete. You might like to finish these yourself.

I feel good when...
What I expect from my teacher is...

I get mad at myself when...
When someone is nice to me I...
I often think about...
If I had a choice, I would...
I feel pleased with myself when...
Tomorrow I would like to...
I like myself best when...
Cooperation is important because...
One way I am like everybody else is...
One way I am different from everybody else is...
Something I do well is...
My best friend...
Something I wish I could do better is...
I worry about...
If I want to I can...

Thursday September 7

DIFFICULT things are put in our way not to stop us, but to call out our courage and our strength.

Author unknown

Friday September 8

MY husband, George, was a great admirer of British prime minister Sir Winston Churchill. I'm sure he would have enjoyed this story.

Lord Moran, for years the personal physician to Churchill, was asked by a reporter how he kept his elderly patient in top physical condition.

"I watch his diet very closely," he replied.

"His diet?" said the reporter, knowing that Churchill ate and drank without restraint.

"Yes," replied the good doctor. "I watch to see what he eats at every meal, and then I order the same thing for myself!"

Saturday September 9

A WOODLAND in full colour is awesome as a forest fire; but a single tree is like the tongue of flame to warm the heart.

Hal Borland

Although the leaves have just begun to turn, we have a small maple in our yard that is already a brilliant red. At any time of the day, when I need a quick pick-me-up, I just go to the window to see that tree. Even on the gray, miserable day, the maple leaves are like a fire, warming my spirit and reminding me of the beauty that is all around us.

Sunday September 10

M AN looketh on the outward appearance, but the Lord looketh on the heart.

Samuel 16:7

Monday September 11

AS any writer knows, there is nothing more disappointing than having a manuscript given back. However, I believe that even I could be happy to be rejected by this Chinese editor.

"Illustrious brother of the sun and moon—behold thy servant prostrate before thy feet. I kowtow to thee and beg of thy graciousness thou mayest grant that I may speak and live. Thy honoured manuscript has deigned to cast the light of its august countenance upon me. With raptures I have pursued it. By the bones of my ancestors, never have I encountered such wit, such pathos, such lofty thoughts. With fear and trembling I return the writing. Were I to publish the treasure you sent me, the Emperor would order that it be made the standard, and that none be published except such as equalled it. Knowing literature as I do, and that it would be impossible in ten thousand years to equal what you have done, I send your writing back. Ten thousand times I crave your pardon. Behold my head is at your feet. Do what you will.

Your servant's servant, The Editor"

Tuesday September 12

THE tints of autumn—a mighty flower garden blossoming under the spell of the enchanter, frost.

John Greenleaf Whittier

Wednesday September 13

The Last Rose of Summer
'Tis the last rose of summer,
Left blooming alone;
All her lovely companions
Are faded and gone;
No flower of her kindred,
No rosebud is nigh,
To reflect back her blushes,
Or give sigh for sigh!

I'll not leave thee, thou lone one,
To pine on the stem;
Since the lovely are sleeping,
Go sleep thou with them.
Thus kindly I scatter
Thy leaves o'er the bed
Where thy mates of the garden
Lie scentless and dead.

Soon may I follow,
When friendships decay,
And from love's shining circle
The gems drop away!
When true hearts lie withered,
And fond ones are flown,
Oh! Who would inhabit
This bleak world alone.

Thomas Moore

Thursday September 14

THIS is the season for fall fairs. These area fairs are usually extremely well attended and parking lots are full to overflowing. Bruce told me this amusing story of a problem at one of the larger exhibitions.

An elderly woman was upset because she couldn't find her car. A number of people offered to look for the car for her. She told her helpers that her car was blue, had a dent in the driver's side door and, as well, she was able to come up with part of the license number. After a lengthy search, a young man told her that he had found a car that seemed to answer the description, but it had a ten-foot extension ladder on the roof.

"Oh, yes," the lady exclaimed, "I forgot about that."

Friday September 15

THIS is the time of the year when fruits and vegetables are bounteous. A friend gave me this very simple recipe for Glazed Peach Pie.

7 large peaches, peeled
1 cup sugar
2 1/2 tbsp. cornstarch
1 baked pie shell

Mash 3 peaches or enough to make 1 cup. Combine mashed peaches, sugar and cornstarch; cook until thick. Cool. Put a small amount of the mashed peach glaze on the pie shell. Slice the remaining peaches and fill the shell. Spoon the remaining glaze over the peaches in the shell. Chill.

Saturday September 16

THE direction in which education starts a man will determine his future life.

Plato

Sunday September 17

TO every thing there is a season, and a time to every purpose under the heaven: a time to be born, and a time to die; a time to plant, and a time to pluck up that which is planted; a time to weep, and a time to laugh; a time to mourn, and a time to dance.

Ecclesiastes 3:1, 2, 4

Monday September 18

I THINK that all of us, at one time or another, have complained about our taxes. Income tax, sales tax, property tax—all are paid with great reluctance.

Many years ago, in Stirling, Western Australia, more than half of the city's taxpayers were in arrears on their property taxes. City officials came up with a unique plan to encourage prompt payment of the taxes.

People who paid their taxes before the deadline had their name put into a large box for a prize drawing. The winner received an all-expenses-paid, overseas vacation for two. The scheme was so successful that several neighbouring councils offered similar incentives.

Although we might hope for that same incentive here, I have a feeling that it is a pointless wish.

Tuesday September 19

M Y friend Jake Frampton dropped by today with his new dog, a lovely little mutt that he acquired this past weekend.

"I picked him up on the side of the road, Edna. He was cold, tired, hungry and he wore no collar. I called the Humane Society and the local vet, but no one has reported him missing. I would certainly return him to his rightful owner, but if no one claims him, I would like to keep him as my own."

Leaving unwanted pets in the country is not unusual, but it is so unkind! I thank the unknown author for these lines that remind us of the unnecessary cruelty that some animals endure.

A dog sits waiting in the cold autumn sun,
Too faithful to leave, to frightened to run.
He's been here for days now with nothing to do,
But sit by the road, waiting for you.

He can't understand why you left him that day,
He thought you and he were stopping to play.
He's sure you'll come back, that's why he stays,
How long will he suffer? How many more
    days?

His legs have grown weak, his throat parched
    and dry,
He's sick now from hunger and falls, with
    a sigh.
He lays down his head and closes his eyes.
I wish you could see how a waiting dog dies.

Wednesday September 20

THESE three rules of life were given to me some years ago. I have found them to be quite useful and so I pass them along to you. The first is "Go," the second, "Keep going," and the third, "Help someone else go."

Thursday September 21

WHEN the sun crosses the plane of the earth's equator on March 21, and again on September 21, night and day are of equal length all over the world. This is known as the vernal equinox.

For us here in North America, it signals the arrival of autumn. Fall, here in Canada, is the most beautiful season.

"Autumn creeps in on moccasins, silent as the glow of the Harvest Moon. Now the nights will have the touch and the smell of the frosty air. Days will have the crisp-leaf rustle of fall as the reds and golds, browns and purples signal another year come to ripeness and to maturity."

Hal Borland

Friday September 22

AUTUMN is when leaves turn slowly from green to brown to gold to litter.

Robert Orben

Saturday September 23

ON a Saturday in late September there is a gathering, in Toronto, of some very special people who share a common bond. "Family Day"—a one-day conference for families of children with cancer—is organized by Families of Children with Cancer, the Hematology/Oncology Program of the Hospital for Sick Children and Camp Oochigeas. It is a casual day for families to get together with old friends (and new), and to attend talks on surviving the stresses of having a child with cancer. The children, meanwhile, have a great day at Camp Ooch!

Families living with childhood cancer are reminded daily of how this illness affects every aspect of family life. The purpose of Family Day is to strengthen family members and to help them cope with the challenge of childhood cancer.

As anyone who has had a child with cancer can tell you, there is a tremendous need for the understanding and support that only a parent-to-parent network can provide. Cancer is a terrifying disease and never more so than when it strikes a child.

Family Day offers outstanding keynote speakers, and workshops designed to provide parents with information, possible coping tips, and direction that will relieve some of the worries that parents face.

While family members attend their activities,

the children are well taken care of by the energetic and caring staff of Camp Oochigeas, at the Crescent School. Crafts, sports, scavenger hunts, initiative tasks, songs and entertainment are provided in age groups of junior, intermediate and senior.

Supplied at no cost to the families, it is a day that can help to prepare all who are involved in this difficult time.

Sunday September 24

CAST me not off in the time of old age; forsake me not when my strength faileth.

Psalm 71:9

Monday September 25

THE best remedy for those who are afraid, lonely or unhappy is to go outside, somewhere where they can be quite alone with heavens, nature, and God. Because only then does one feel that all is as it should be and that God wishes to see people happy, amidst the simple beauty of nature. As long as this exists, and it certainly always will, I know that then there will always be comfort for every sorrow, whatever the circumstances may be.

Anne Frank

Tuesday September 26

MARG and I came across an old magazine, tucked away in a box in the basement. What fun we had reading *The Literary Digest* for July 1, 1916. I was particularly intrigued by some of the advertisements. Kellogg's Toasted Corn Flakes, The Liberty Car (from Liberty Motor Car Company), Kelly-Springfield hand-made automobile tires, and O-Cedar furniture polish were just some of the advertisers in the magazine.

The ad that most intrigued me, however, was one for "The Dover Electric Iron."

"The Dover Electric Iron stays HOT even when you are working with heavy wet linens. And all parts of the iron surface are heated equally. The Dover is the result of a 22-year study of the ironing needs of the women of America. It is the dependable, trouble-proof, everlasting iron for which alert housewives have been longing.

"Get a Dover from your dealer today and use it all your life.

"The price, $3.50, is no indication of the Dover's value. There is nothing to compare with it. If your dealer cannot supply you, write us at Dover Manufacturing Co., Dover, Ohio."

A well-to-do neighbour of ours owned a Dover and she was the envy of our neighbourhood. What memories!

Wednesday September 27

MY daughter and I have always enjoyed making our own jams, jellies, chili relish and spaghetti sauce. Most often we have taken on the job of boiling jars and lids, and preserving the fruits and vegetables at this time of year. It is a time-consuming chore, often taking many hours and consecutive days. I recently learned of another way to spread the task over a longer period of time.

A friend of mine offered this suggestion. Wash and freeze whole berries, seedless grapes, pitted plums and sliced apples, peaches and pears, during the summer and fall. It is then possible to wait until winter to cook the fruit down to make the jams and jellies.

The benefits of cooking in winter are three-fold. Prices for sugar, pectin and jars are usually lower in winter; the heat from the kitchen will spread warmth through the house; friends and family may have more time to help out in the winter months than in the fall when there is so much to do outdoors.

I think that I shall try this plan and see how well it works!

Thursday September 28

YOU must have long-range goals to keep from being frustrated by short-range failures.

Charles C. Noble

Friday September 29

WE come closest to God at our lowest moments. It's easier to hear God when you are stripped of arrogance and pride, when you have nothing to rely on except God. It's pretty painful to get to that point, but when you do, God's there.

Terry Anderson

Saturday September 30

THE glory of the star, the glory of the sun— we must not lose either in the other. We must not be so full of the hope of heaven that we cannot do our work on the earth; we must not be so lost in the work of the earth that we shall not be inspired by the hope of heaven.

Phillips Brooks

October

Sunday October 1

For the Blessings of Harvest

ALMIGHTY Father, who hast watered our fields with the dew of heaven, and poured out upon us the former and the latter rain, according to our need, and hast reserved unto us the appointed weeks of the harvest: We bless and praise thee that, in love to thy children, thou hast at this season bestowed upon us such an abundant supply for all our necessities. Grant that we may not be destitute of those better gifts which nourish and enrich the soul. Pour down, we beseech thee, upon us thy heavenly grace, and endow us with the gifts of thy Holy Spirit, that we may bring forth abundant fruits to do thy glory; through Jesus Christ our Lord. Amen.

The Book of Common Prayer

Monday October 2

The autumn frosts will lie upon the grass
Like bloom on grapes of purple-brown
  and gold.

The misted early mornings will be cold;
The little puddles will be roofed with glass.

Elinor Wylie

Tuesday October 3

LET us reconcile ourselves to the mysterious rhythm of our destinies. Let us treasure our joys, but not bewail our sorrows. The glory of light cannot exist without its shadows. Life is a whole, and good and ill must be accepted together. The journey has been enjoyable and well worth making—once.

Winston Churchill

Wednesday October 4

WHAT do Yogi Berra, former baseball player and coach, and Samuel Goldwyn, film-maker extraordinaire, have in common? Between them they have managed to create many wise—if mangled—contributions to our English language. Here are just a few of the duo's malapropisms that have made us laugh over the years.

From Samuel Goldwyn
A verbal contract isn't worth the paper it's written on.
We're overpaying him, but he's worth it.

I'll give you a definite maybe.
A bachelor's life is no life for a single man.
Don't talk to me while I'm interrupting.

From Yogi Berra
It ain't over 'til it's over.
No wonder nobody comes here, it's too crowded.
It's tough to play left field in Yankee Stadium, because it gets late early.
If you can't imitate him, don't copy him.

Thursday October 5

IF everything were to turn out just like I would want it to, then I would never experience anything new; my life would be an endless repetition of stale successes.

Hugh Prather

Friday October 6

KINDNESS! What a wonderful word. When we do a generous deed for someone without any thought of what we'll get in return, it can become a chain reaction of goodwill. Each act of kindness rewards us by making us feel better, and it reminds us of what is really important in life.

Consider some of the simple things that can be done each day.

Let someone go ahead of you in line.
Hold a door open for someone.
Sign an organ donor card.
Plant a tree.
Visit with an elderly neighbour.
Donate blood.
Volunteer at your local school.
Send a friend a greeting card for no reason.
Smile more often.

Remember: every time we help one another, we make the world a better place.

Saturday October 7

THIS is Thanksgiving weekend here in Canada. I think these words from J.E. Anderson are most appropriate for today.

For the Fruits of Harvest

I'm grateful at this time of year
For all the golden grain,
For all the fruits at harvest time,
For sunshine and for rain.

For every blessing known to man,
And every lovely flower,
For each and every friend I have,
And every golden hour.

I'm grateful, too, for every child,
For every starry night,
For music, health and happiness,
For morning's promise bright.

I'm grateful for the path to choose
For weary feet to trod,
And to ascend the heights sublime
Yes, hand in hand with God.

Sunday October 8

O GIVE thanks unto the Lord; for he is good: for his mercy endureth for ever.

Psalm 136:1

Monday October 9

Thanksgiving Day

FROM the time that the first settlers arrived in Canada, early October has been the time when families paused, after the harvest, to give thanks for all good things given to us. Although each family celebrates in its own way, it will most often celebrate together.

We McCanns are no exception. Although we are widely scattered across the country, nearly all family members will be here to enjoy the Thanksgiving get-together.

Getting the turkey ready today is as simple as removing the plastic wrap covering, taking out the nicely packaged giblets, adding the stuffing and placing the bird in the oven. Some people, who consider this to be a "chore," will be interested in reading these instructions, taken from an old family cookbook.

"Select a young turkey; remove all of the feathers carefully; singe the bird over a burning newspaper on the top of the stove; then "draw" it nicely, being very careful not to break any of the internal organs. Remove the crop carefully; cut off the neck close to the body. Rinse out the inside of the turkey several times and in the next to last rinse mix in a teaspoon of baking soda. Rinse again, and then wipe the turkey dry inside and out, with a clean cloth. Rub the inside with some salt, then stuff the breast and body with 'Dressing for Fowls.'"

I think we may be very thankful for an easier holiday dinner.

Tuesday October 10

AS the baseball season moves into the play-offs, the sports writers will be voting to determine the winners of the many post season awards. One of the most prestigious awards is the Cy Young Award, given to the best pitcher in both the American and the National Leagues.

Many sports fans may not know of the amazing feats of Denton "Cy" Young. Born in Ohio in 1867, he spent every spare minute, when not helping on the family farm, pitching baseball. In 1890, while he was warming up his pitching arm, several errant balls struck a fence. A sports writer, looking at the splintered wood, remarked, "It looked like a cyclone struck 'em." Thus came the nickname that would stay with him for his entire career and come to signify pitching excellence.

In his pro career, Cy threw for 20 or more wins in 14 consecutive seasons, five seasons of 30 or more and three no-hitters (one a perfect game). His 511 wins will likely never be equalled.

Retired in 1912, he was inducted into the Baseball Hall of Fame in 1937. Shortly after his passing in 1955, baseball established the Cy Young Award to honour the outstanding pitchers in each season.

Wednesday October 11

WOMEN have a favourite room, men a favourite chair.

Thursday October 12

ON these chilly evenings, I often enjoy a hot bowl of soup and rolls for my evening meal.

Here's a favourite recipe for delicious and easy-to-make rolls.

Onion-Bacon Rolls
8 bacon slices
1 small onion
1 small green bell pepper, diced
1/2 tsp. dried dillweed
1/2 tsp. pepper
1 tsp. dried parsley flakes
1 package (16oz.) frozen roll dough, thawed
1/4 cup milk
1 tsp. sesame seeds
1 tsp. poppy seeds

Preheat oven to 375°F. Cook bacon in a large skillet until crisp; remove bacon, reserving 1 tbsp. drippings in the skillet. Crumble the bacon. Sauté the diced onion and bell pepper in drippings until tender; remove with a slotted spoon, and drain on paper towels. Place mixture in a bowl; stir in bacon, dillweed, pepper and parsley flakes. Pat each roll into a three-inch circle; spoon 1 tbsp. of the bacon mixture in the centre. Bring up the edges, pinching to seal; place seam side down into lightly greased muffin pans. Brush rolls with milk, sprinkle with poppy seeds and sesame seeds. Cover and let rise in a warm place, free from drafts, for 30 minutes—or until double in bulk. Bake for 15 minutes until golden. Yields 2 dozen.

Friday October 13

DO you feel a little edgy today? If you are nervous because it is a Friday and the date is the thirteenth, you may be suffering from *triskaidekaphobia*. Experts offer the opinion that this fear stems from the fact that there were thirteen people at the Last Supper and that Christ's crucifixion occurred on a Friday. Whatever the cause of the fear, there will be a number of people who will venture very cautiously into this day.

Saturday October 14

HERE are a few things to remember:

The value of time,
The pleasure of working,
The worth of character,
The virtue of patience,
The wisdom of economy,
The obligation of duty,
The power of a smile,
The profit of experience,
The strength of perseverance,
The joy of achievement.

Sunday October 15

HOW shall a young man steer an honest course? By holding to thy word. With my whole heart I strive to find thee; let me not stray from thy commandments.

Psalm 119:9–10

Monday October 16

WATCHING the runners from the high school running team go by our home today brought back a memory from almost twenty years ago. Two of the young runners were wearing shirts showing that they had participated in the Terry Fox Run.

I have always admired those who show courage in the face of adversity and I know of no one who exemplified bravery more than Terry Fox.

Losing a leg to cancer could have made this young athlete angry and bitter. He did become angry, not at his loss, but at the disease that caused it. In an effort to raise funds for research into the dreaded disease, he decided to run across the country, from Newfoundland to British Columbia.

The fundraiser started slowly, but by the time he reached Ontario, people came by the thousands to cheer him on and to donate generously to his noble cause.

I will never forget seeing this slightly built young man as he ran-hopped by me on a warm summer's morning in Muskoka.

Although Terry had a recurrence of cancer and was forced to stop his cross-country marathon in Thunder Bay, his run to raise funds has never ended. Terry succumbed to cancer in 1981, but the Terry Fox Run to raise funds for research has carried on every year since his death.

I found this tribute in *The Globe and Mail*, July 1, 1981, to be a particularly poignant tribute:

"Terry Fox's race is over. In fact he never finished the course, none of us do. What is important is to set goals. What is important is not to quit, not ever. What is important is to run well and honestly, with as much human grace as possible—not forgetting, too, to take joy in the running."

Tuesday October 17

OF all the joys that lighten suffering on earth, what joy is welcome like a newborn child.

C. Norton

Wednesday October 18

"THE budget should be balanced, the treasury should be refilled, public debt should be reduced, the arrogance of officialdom should be tempered and controlled, and assistance to foreign lands should be reduced lest the state become bankrupt. The people should be forced to work and not just depend on government for subsistence."

Is this a platform from the leaders of our government? You might possibly think so, but in fact, these wise thoughts are from Cicero (106–43 B.C.).

The more things change, the more they stay the same.

Thursday October 19

The Gold October Day

The wind blows through the aspens
This gold October day,
Limber of trunk and gracious,
See how they lean and sway.

Their leaves are all aflutter,
A trembling lot they are...
Like golden coins they glimmer...
I see them from afar.

Without the least resistance
They yield to autumn's whims,
Till every leaf has fallen
And left but barren limbs.

So here I stand to gather
Gems from autumn's bouquet...
While winds blow through the aspens,
This gold October day!

Georgia B. Adams

Friday October 20

THE idle man does not know what it is to enjoy rest. Hard work, moreover, not only tends to give us rest for the body, but what is even more important, peace to the soul.

Sir John Lubbock

Saturday October 21

MY friends Will and Muriel are babysitting their grandchildren this weekend. Their children live out of town, so Will and Muriel don't see their grandchildren as frequently as they would like. This makes the time spent together even more special.

Some grandparents don't have the same problem, and this is illustrated by the amusing story that Will told me this morning.

"Dear," said the voice on the telephone when the young woman answered, "this is Mom. I'm calling to find out if Dad and I could leave the children with you and Jim tonight. We've been invited out for the evening."

Sunday October 22

I WILL hear what the Lord God will say: for he shall speak peace unto his people and to his saints, and unto them that turn their heart to him.

Psalm 85:8

Monday October 23

THOSE who love deeply never grow old; they may die of old age, but they die young.

Sir Arthur Wing Pinero

Thursday October 24

WHAT is more cheerful, now, in the fall of the year, than an open-wood fire? Do you hear those little chirps and twitters coming out of that piece of apple-wood? Those are the ghosts of the robins and bluebirds that sang upon the bough when it was in blossom last spring. In summer, whole flocks of them come fluttering about the fruit trees under the window: so I have singing birds all year round.

Thomas Bailey Aldrich

Wednesday October 25

THOUGH a little one, the master word "work" looms large in meaning. It is the open sesame to every portal, the great equalizer in the world, the true philosopher's stone which transmits all the base metal of humanity into gold.

Sir William Osler

Thursday October 26

TRUE friendship is like sound health; the value of it is seldom known until it is lost.

Charles Colton

Friday October 27

NO matter what happens, there's always someone who knew it would.

Saturday October 28

It's nice to have a faithful friend
In whom I may confide,
Who stands beside me with his trust
Through low may be the tide.
It's also nice to be of help
When he, too, has a need—
But friendship isn't made of words
But by each loving deed.

Author unknown

Sunday October 29

THOU visitest the earth and blessest it: thou makest it very plenteous. The river of God is full of water: thou preparest their corn, for so thou providest for the earth. Thou crownest the year with thy goodness: and thy clouds drop fatness.

Psalm 65:9, 11

Monday October 30

APOLOGIZING for a nasty remark is like trying to unscramble an egg.

Wednesday October 31

HALLOWEEN is one of the very oldest holidays, tracing its origins back thousands of years. The holiday we know as Halloween has had a multitude of influences from many cultures.

The ultimate origins came from the ancient Celtic harvest festival "Samhain," a time when people believed that the spirits of the dead roamed the earth. It was a three-day festival, and many people would wear costumes made from animal skins.

When Romans invaded Britain in the first century, they brought the tradition of "Pomona Day," a celebration for the goddess of fruits and vegetables that was held on November 1. With the spread of Christianity, November 1 became "All Saints' Day." November 2, "All Souls' Day," honoured the dead with bonfires and parades. People wore costumes as saints, angels and devils.

The Halloween that we celebrate today is a combination of all these influences: Pomona Day's harvest treats, Samhain's black cats, magic and evil spirits and the ghosts, skeletons and skulls from All Saints' Day and All Souls' Day.

The original jack-o-lanterns were carved by the Celts out of big turnips. Early settlers in America found the pumpkin to be larger and more colourful, and it soon replaced the turnip as the jack-o-lantern—the most widely recognized symbol of Halloween.

Following the ongoing tradition, our neighbourhood trick-or-treaters will arrive soon. I look forward to their visit.

November

Wednesday November 1

All Saints' Day

A LITTLE child on a summer morning stood in a great cathedral church. The sunlight streamed through the beautiful stained-glass windows, and the figures in them of the servants of God were a bright and brilliant colour. A little later the question was asked, "What is a saint?" and the child replied, "A saint is a person who lets the light shine through."

Our minister tells us that a saint is an ordinary believer in God, who, on his or her journey through life, has lived the faith by being concerned about others.

There are so many "saints" who have touched my life—a patient school teacher, a kind neighbour's child who shovelled the driveway, a nurse in the hospital who came into my room in the middle of the night when she knew that I couldn't sleep.

I thank them all!

Thursday November 2

Day is done, gone the sun,
From the lake, from the hills, from the sky.
All is well. Safely rest. God is nigh.

Fading light, end the sight.
And a star gems the night, gleaming bright.
From afar, drawing nigh, falls the night.

From "Taps" by Daniel Butterfield

Friday November 3

IWOULD rather go to the forest, far away and build me a little cabin—build it myself—and daub it with clay, and live there with my wife and children; and have a winding path leading down to the spring where the water bubbles out, day and night, whispering a poem to the white pebbles, from the heart of the earth; a little hut with some hollyhocks at the corner, with their bannered bosoms open to the sun, and a thrush in the air like a winged joy—I would rather live there and have some lattice-work across the window so that the sunlight would fall checkered on the babe in the cradle—I would rather live free, than in a palace of gold, and wear a crown of imperial power, and feel that I was superstition's cringing slave, and dare not speak my honest thought.

Robert G. Ingersoll

Saturday November 4

MY son-in-law Bruce is an avid football fan, and for many years his favourite team has been the Toronto Argonauts.

One of the finest players ever to wear the "double blue" is an amazing man both on and off the field. Michael "Pinball" Clemons doesn't look like a football player. Just five-foot–six-inches tall, and with a smile almost that wide, his shy, unassuming demeanor belies his competitive spirit and the heart of a true champion.

Born in Florida in 1965, Michael Luttrell Clemons was raised by his mother (his enduring strength and example) in the projects of his hometown, Dunedin. An excellent student, he also excelled at sports, first playing football at eight years of age. He quickly developed the knack of eluding larger tacklers with a combination of speed and tremendous lateral motion. His academic and football abilities earned him a scholarship to the College of William and Mary, in Virginia.

After a short stint in the NFL, Clemons came to Canada—and the Toronto Argonauts. Touted by the coach as a player who "bounces around like a pinball," the press picked up the name and he was "The Pinball" forevermore.

His football statistics are well known: 3,300 yards rushing in a single season, Player of the Year, Grey Cup winner. These are just a few of the honours that he has earned.

Even more impressive to me are his off-field activities. He works with numerous charities, such as the Canadian Cancer Society, the United Way, the Red Shield Appeal, the Juvenile Diabetes Foundation and the Special Olympics. This thought is taken from his book, *All Heart*.

"Michael's life on the field is only one small part of who he is. His heart embraces his family—wife Dianne and daughters Rachel and Raven. His heart embraces youth, the disabled, and the underprivileged. He inspires good works by example. He teaches youth to make sound decisions. He calls people to be strong in their faith, for God has been Michael's rock and the Lord his guide."

Sunday November 5

A FAITHFUL friend is a strong defence: and he that hath found such an one hath found a treasure.

Ecclesiasticus 4:31

Monday November 6

THANKS to the alertness of the sportscasters and miracles of modern communication, it is often possible to know the score of every major football game in the country—except the one to which you are listening.

Bill Vaughan

Tuesday November 7

Friendship is a golden chain,
The links are friends so dear,
And like a rare and precious jewel
It's treasured more each year.

It's clasped together firmly
With a love that's deep and true,
And it's rich with happy memories
And fond recollections too.

Time can't destroy its beauty
For, as long as memory lives,
Years can't erase the pleasure
That the joy of friendship gives.

For friendship is a priceless gift,
That can't be bought or sold,
But to have an understanding friend
Is worth far more than gold.

And the golden chain of friendship
Is a strong and blessed tie
Binding kindred hearts together
As the years go passing by.

Author unknown

Wednesday November 8

THE deeper man goes into life, the deeper is his conviction that this life is not all; it is an "unfinished symphony." A day may round out an insect's life, and a bird or a beast needs no tomorrow. Not so with him who knows that he is related to God and has felt the power of an endless life.

Henry Ward Beecher

Thursday November 9

IN the best of times, our days are numbered anyway. It would be a crime against nature for any generation that it put off enjoying those things for which we were presumably designed in the first place—the opportunity to do good work, to fall in love, to enjoy friends, to hit a ball, to bounce a baby.

Alistair Cooke

Friday November 10

WE had our first brief taste of winter weather today with some freezing rain. No matter when it comes, the first day of winter driving seems to catch us unawares. It's as if the beautiful summer weather has erased all memory of how to drive in ice and snow. Experts offer these important tips for safe driving in difficult weather.

One of the most important reminders for winter driving is also the most often forgotten: slow down! You have much greater control over your car if you are moving more slowly.

In a skid, the majority of people will hit the brakes. In fact, you should take your foot off the brake and steer in the direction of the skid. Shifting into a lower gear, even in a car with automatic transmission, can also slow progress without locking up your wheels and steering wheel.

Remember, it is a long season. Be careful and arrive safely.

Saturday November 11

Remembrance Day

THESE heroes are dead. They died for liberty—they died for us. They are at rest. They sleep in the land they made free, under the flag they rendered stainless, under the solemn pines, the sad hemlocks, the tearful willows, the embracing vines. They sleep beneath the shadow of the clouds, careless alike of sunshine and a storm, each in the windowless palace of rest. Earth may run red with other wars—they are at peace. In the midst of battles, in the roar of conflicts, they found the serenity of death.

Robert G. Ingersoll

At the eleventh hour of the eleventh day of the eleventh month, 1918, the armistice between the Allied and Central Powers was signed, ending the First World War. To honour the memory of the soldiers who died defending our country, we observe a two-minute silence at 11 a.m., the hour at which the hostilities ended.

Although it is a long time since the Second World War ended, there are those of us whose memories of those dark days remain vivid. We who lost family members or friends will pause today and remember with grateful thanks those men and women who paid the ultimate price.

It is my fondest hope that those whose memories do not stretch to those days of war may be grateful for the peace that has been provided for them.

Sunday November 12

The Collect for Remembrance Day

MOST merciful Father, who hast been pleased to take unto thyself our brethren departed: grant to us who are still in our pilgrimage, and who walk as yet by faith, that having served thee faithfully in this world, we may, with all faithful Christian souls, be joined hereafter to the company of thy blessed Saints in glory; through Jesus Christ our Lord, who with thee and that Holy Spirit liveth and reigneth, one God, world without end. Amen.

The Book of Common Prayer

Monday November 13

MY great-grandson, Michael, seems prone to ear infections. Having had many earaches as a child myself, I sympathize with him. Jamie has found something that seems to be very comforting to Michael when he is suffering. She half-fills a clean sock with rice and knots the top. She then places the sock in the microwave oven on high for about 30 seconds. After checking to be sure that the sock isn't too hot, she places the sock on Michael's sore ear. The warmth and the pressure seem to provide great comfort.

Of course this doesn't take the place of a visit to the doctor, but it does keep Michael slightly more comfortable until the appointment can be made.

Tuesday November 14

IN life there is nothing more unexpected and surprising than the arrivals and departures of pleasure. If we find it in one place today, it is vain to seek it there tomorrow. You cannot lay a trap for it.

Alexander Smith

Wednesday November 15

IDEALS are like stars; you will not succeed on touching them with your hands. But like the seafaring man on the desert of waters, you choose them as your guides, and following them you will reach your destiny.

Carl Schurz

Thursday November 16

ENGLISHMAN Thomas Hood describes November this way.

No warmth nor cheer nor ease,
No comfortable feel in any member
No shade, no shine, no butterflies, no bees,
No fruits, no flowers, no leaves, no birds,
   No-vember.

I think many of us feel the same way about this dreariest of all months. I do have my own remedy, however, and I recommend it to all. A cozy fireplace, a good book, a comfortable chair and quiet music all help me to escape the gray days of November.

Friday November 17

MY daughter Julia recently returned from a trip to Switzerland. She brought back with her a delectable recipe for Fondue Neuchâteloise, which we enjoyed this evening. Julia also told us the story of the origin of this delicious meal.

In Neuchâtel it is said that the cheese fondue was invented by the *vigeronnes*—wives of the wine growers of the hills around the town. During the harvest, the *vigeronnes* had to work so hard helping with the grape picking that they had no time to cook an evening meal. To prepare a quick and nourishing dish, they melted cheese in wine. Fondue is also found in one form or another everywhere in the Alps.

Fondue Neuchâteloise
2 cloves garlic
8 oz. Emmenthaler cheese
8 oz. Gruyere cheese
1 1/2 cups white wine
1 tsp. cornstarch
1 small glass of Kirsch
fresh ground pepper to taste
French bread cut into squares

Fondue is prepared at the table over a flame, in a *caquelon*—a kind of earthenware pot with a handle. Rub the pot with the cloves of garlic. Grate the cheeses into the pot. Add the wine and very slowly bring just to the boiling point, stirring continuously with a wooden spoon. (Julia suggests that best results are obtained by constantly tracing a figure 8 on the bottom of the pot.) Mix the cornstarch with the Kirsch. Add the mixture when the fondue begins to simmer. Grind in pepper to taste. Pick up pieces of bread on long fondue forks and dip into the fondue, again using the figure 8. Keep the fondue very hot.

The tradition is that a person who loses a piece of bread in the fondue is supposed to pay for the next bottle of wine or to organize the next fondue party.

Saturday November 18

WHAT we usually pray to God is not that his will be done, but that he approve ours.

H. B. Gross

Sunday November 19

THE scriptures teach us the best way of living, the noblest way of suffering, and the most comfortable way of dying.

Flavel

Monday November 20

GRAY hairs seem to my fancy like the sort of light of the moon, silvering over the evening of life.

Jean Paul Frederich Richter

Tuesday November 21

PHYLLIS and Bill suffered the loss of a very close friend this past weekend. Chris had waged a valiant battle against cancer, and, although his death was a blessed relief from his suffering, it was, nonetheless, a tragic loss to his family and many friends.

I hope that this poem from Robert Louis Stevenson will provide a small measure of comfort.

He is not dead, this friend; not dead
But, in the path we mortals tread
Gone some few, trifling steps ahead,
And nearer to the end;
So that you, too, once past the bend,
Shall meet again, as face to face, this friend
You fancy dead.

Wednesday November 22

FORTY is the old age of youth, fifty the youth of old age.

Victor Hugo

Thursday November 23

TODAY is the day when our American neighbours celebrate Thanksgiving. The first Thanksgiving Proclamation was made by Governor Bradford, three years after the Pilgrims settled in Plymouth.

To All Ye Pilgrims

Inasmuch as the great Father has given us this year an abundant harvest of Indian corn, wheat, peas, beans, squashes and garden vegetables and has made the forests to abound with game and the sea with fish and clams, and inasmuch as he has protected us from the ravages of savages, has spared us from pestilence and disease, has granted us freedom to worship God according to the dictates of our own conscience; now I, your magistrate, do proclaim that all ye Pilgrims with your wives and ye little ones do gather at the meeting house, on ye hill between the hours of 9 and 12 in the daytime, on Thursday November ye 29th of the year of our Lord 1623, and in the third year since ye Pilgrims landed on ye Pilgrim Rock, there to listen to ye pastor and render thanksgiving to ye Almighty God for all his blessings.

Friday November 24

WHEN something goes wrong, it is important to talk, not about who is to blame, but about who is going to fix it.

Saturday November 25

JAKE Frampton mentioned today that his father believed in stern discipline. "When I did something wrong, he provided the discipline and I provided the stern!"

Sunday November 26

WE know that all things work together for good to them that love God, to them who are called according to his purpose.

Romans 8:28

Monday November 27

YOU cannot help men permanently by doing for them what they could, and should, do for themselves.

Tuesday November 28

MY son-in-law John, a minister, likes to keep his sermons short and to the point. He cites as the reason advice given to him early in his career: "A wise minister told me that if you can't get the idea of a sermon in ten minutes, it isn't worth half an hour. Sermons should be measured by strength—not length."

Wednesday November 29

HE is rich who owns the day, and no one owns the day who allows it to be invaded by worry, fret and anxiety.

Ralph Waldo Emerson

Thursday November 30

GO to your friend for sympathy; that is natural. Go to your books for comfort, for counsel. But the time will come when no book, no friend, can decide your problem for you; when nothing can help you, nothing can save you, but yourself. Begin now to stand alone.

Angela Morgan

December

Friday December 1

THIS evening as I looked out on the snow falling gently, I was reminded of these lines from Grace Noll Crowell.

A Wintry Mile

Walk a mile in the winter twilight,
Mark its whiteness and breathe its cold,
Reach your hand to the sunset embers,
Warm them then and when you are old
There will be times when you will recall it:
A beautiful, perfect, shining while,
That will glow in your heart like a splendid
    diamond—
You will remember that winter mile.

You will recall the clean cold stinging
Of winter wind on your throat and lips;
The lift of your heart in its youthful gladness,
The tingle of blood to your fingertips;
You will have drawn to your heart forever
This hour, the snow, the light in the west—
Walk a while in the winter twilight,
Store its treasure within your breast.

Saturday December 2

MY friend Emily is visiting with friends in Albuquerque, New Mexico. This past week, they spent several days preparing the *luminarias* or "lights of Christmas" for the traditional Christmas Eve lighting of the city. Emily wrote to me.

"This custom originated in Spain where the first *luminarias* were bonfires made from criss-crossed pine boughs piled into three-foot-high squares. When coloured wrapping paper came to Spain from the Orient, people chose to make coloured lanterns and string them through the trees and around their houses.

As Spanish people emigrated to Mexico, and then into the southwestern United States, they brought the custom with them.

In 1802, Yankee traders brought brown paper bags in their supplies for the immigrants, and bags have been used in place of the lanterns ever since.

In villages all over New Mexico, haciendas, adobe huts, sidewalks and streets are outlined with *luminarias*, and every other light in town is turned off. The sight is so spectacular that people come to New Mexico just to see the lights.

To make a *luminaria*, you use a paper grocery bag with two-inch cuff folded down at the top. Fill the bottom of the bag with 2 to 3 inches of sand. Place a candle securely in the center of the sand, and you are finished.

We made nearly 100 *luminarias* and I can hardly wait until Christmas Eve!"

Sunday December 3

First Sunday in Advent

Hark the glad sound! the Saviour comes,
The Saviour promised long:
Let every heart prepare a throne,
And every voice a song.

Our glad hosannas, Prince of Peace
Thy welcome shall proclaim;
And heaven's eternal arches ring
With thy beloved name.

Rev. P. Doddbridge

Monday December 4

DURING the four weeks of Advent, the period of preparation for Christ's coming, we celebrate with services and devotions at church and in our home. Many of the Advent traditions came to North America from Europe.

The circular shape of the wreath, the candles and the Advent calendar are all now adopted here in North America.

In our family we like to enjoy a special meal on the first Sunday in Advent. Each person in the family is given a chance to pick something that they particularly want. This often leads to a rather strange and unique combination of foods, but it seems to make the dinner more memorable.

Tuesday December 5

ADVICE is like snow—the softer it falls, the longer it dwells upon and the deeper it sinks into the mind.

Samuel Taylor Coleridge

Wednesday December 6

HE who has health has hope, and he who has hope, has everything.

Arabian Proverb

Thursday December 7

GIVE us the strength to encounter that which is to come, that we may be brave in peril, constant in all changes of fortune, and down to the dates of death, loyal and loving one to another.

Robert Louis Stevenson

Friday December 8

W HEN we seek to discover the best in others, we somehow bring out the best in ourselves.

William Arther Ward

Saturday December 9

M ANY of us who live on a fixed budget need to be very creative when it comes to gift-giving at Christmas. This year Lila and I have made presents that we hope will please all who receive them.

During our neighbourhood walks this fall, we collected bags of pine cones—hundreds of cones. We purchased a number of inexpensive baskets and strings of white mini-lights along with several metres of Christmas ribbon.

In each basket we glued pine cones of varying sizes. As we placed the cones in the basket, we wound a string of lights through the cones, leaving many of the lights on the top of the cones.

On some of the baskets, we sprinkled a bit of glitter; on others we spray-painted some of the cones in gold and silver.

When everything was dried, we added a bright bow of coloured ribbon. The finished product makes a lovely centrepiece for any table. As well, a change of ribbon may let it be used for Easter or even outside on a patio in the summer.

Lila and I are thrilled with our gifts—and our ingenuity.

Sunday December 10

Second Sunday in Advent

Rejoice, Rejoice, Emmanuel shall come to thee, O Israel.

Traditional carol from 9th century Latin

Monday December 11

AT this time of year, unexpected company is a frequent occurrence. It's always nice to have a few tried-and-true snack foods on hand that you can pull together on short notice.

Bonnie Gosse, a lovely young friend of mine, gave me this recipe for salmon dip. Bonnie is very health conscious and has done her level best to make me so as well. I hope that it pleases her that this low-fat, healthy snack is one of my favourites.

Super Salmon Dip

1 can (7 oz.) red Sockeye salmon, drained, with bones and skin removed.

1 package (8 oz.) light cream cheese, softened

1 tsp. garlic, minced

1 tsp. lemon juice

1 tbsp. Worcestershire sauce
1 tbsp parsley, chopped
parsley sprigs for garnish

Lightly mash the salmon with a fork to break into small pieces. Place softened cream cheese in a medium-sized bowl. Add salmon, garlic, lemon juice, Worcestershire sauce and parsley. Blend together well with a fork.

Cover the bowl with plastic and refrigerate until about an hour before serving. Decorate the serving bowl with sprigs of parsley and serve with a basket of low-fat wheat crackers.

Tuesday December 12

AN activity that our family enjoys at this time of year is "Christmas movie night" (or nights, as there are so many outstanding seasonal films).

My favourite of the old films is the 1951 version of Charles Dickens' *A Christmas Carol*. Alistair Sims was critically acclaimed for his brilliant portrayal of Mr. Scrooge, and even the youngest of our family members love this most famous of Christmas films. Others of our favourites are *It's a Wonderful Life*, the 1946 movie starring Jimmy Stewart and Donna Reed, *Miracle on 34th Street*, and *Holiday Inn*, where Bing Crosby sings the immortal Irving Berlin song, "White Christmas."

A movie night can provide an evening of relaxation at a very busy time of year.

Wednesday December 13

The Christmas cards and letters
  with messages of cheer
Renew the bonds of friendship
  neglected through the year.
They bring a sense of nearness,
  a unity that gives
A oneness of the spirit
  in fellowship that lives.

Author unknown

I finished the last of my cards today, just before the postal deadline for mailing. This is a tradition that I love!

Thursday December 14

FOR many people, Christmas is not the happiest time of year. It can be a time when friends living in nursing homes feel forgotten. Making time in our busy schedules to stop in with a card, a poinsettia or a Christmas candle is important.

Make someone else's day happier and you are sure to have brightened your own.

Friday December 15

A GOOD man doubles the length of his existence. To have lived so as to look back with pleasure on life is to have lived twice.

Author unknown

Saturday December 16

WE are often tempted by delicious rich food at this time of year. Each time I hear Bruce groan about his waistline, I remember a good friend who decided she should lose some weight. She sent away for a diet program recommended in a magazine.

After reading it, she threw it away in disgust. "For gracious sake," she said, "they try to make you cut down on your food!"

Sunday December 17

Third Sunday in Advent

O Christmas tree, O Christmas tree,
You come from God, eternal.
A symbol of the Lord of Love
Whom God to man sent from above.
O Christmas tree, O Christmas tree,
You come from God eternal.

Traditional German carol

Monday December 18

EIGHTY-SEVEN years ago yesterday, Orville Wright made the first flight in an airplane. It wasn't much—a hundred and twenty feet, and lasting but twelve seconds—but it was the success of a dream shared by the two brothers, Orville and Wilbur.

Dreams of flying had been a part of life for centuries. Leonardo da Vinci, in the fifteenth century, tried to develop flying equipment, and said this: "For once you have tasted flight, you will walk the earth with your eyes turned skyward, for there you have been and there you long to return."

Tuesday December 19

IN winters past, the sound of jingling bells and laughter often filled the frosty air. On snowy evenings families would climb into their horse-drawn sleighs and enjoy a ride.

Although those days are long past, many of the "pioneer villages" still offer rides in the old-time horse-drawn sleighs. Perhaps you could make this a gift to your grandchildren or great-grandchildren. It's certainly something they wouldn't soon forget.

Wednesday December 20

Of all the things you wear, your expression is the most important.

Thursday December 21

Christmas comes but once a year
But when it comes, it brings good cheer.

How true that proverb is! Julia and I went shopping today, and it seemed that everyone we met was smiling. I'm not sure whether it is the lovely decorations that we see everywhere, or the look on the children's faces as they sit on Santa's knee that brings the smile to my face. Whatever it is, the Christmas feeling seems to gladden all our hearts.

Friday December 22

HANUKKAH, or the "Festival of Lights," is observed each year about this time. It celebrates Jerusalem's return to the worship of God from Greek Syrian paganism, in the year 165 B.C. This festival is possibly the most widely celebrated holiday in Jewish homes. Long before the Christian observance of Christmas, Hanukkah was an exciting and joyous time for Jewish children. For the modern Jewish person,

Hanukkah is much more than candle-lighting, and gift-giving to children. It is the knowledge and resolve that every human being—in every part of the world—must be free to worship in the way they choose.

One of the foods often served at Hanukkah celebrations is the latke, a potato pancake. This recipe comes to you from my dear friend Esther Schwartz.

> 2 cups uncooked potatoes, coarsely grated
> 2 eggs, separated
> 1 tsp. salt
> 1 tbsp. (rounded) flour or matzo meal
> 1 onion, grated
> 1/8 cup vegetable oil

Combine potatoes, egg yolks, salt, flour and onion. Beat egg whites and fold into the mixture. Heat oil in a medium-sized skillet until it sizzles. Drop mixture by the spoonful into the skillet. Fry latkes on both sides until golden brown. Drain on paper towels. Serve hot with sour cream, apple-sauce or both.

Saturday December 23

FOR many people, today is a time for last-minute shopping. Since Marg and I had finished all of our shopping and wrapping, we spent the day putting finishing touches on the dinner table. When the silver had been polished and the crystal and china set in place, Marg and I made a cup of tea and took out some old Christmas photo albums.

What a wonderful time we had! Each and every picture evoked enjoyable memories of our loved ones and of Christmases past. It was a reminder of how lucky we are to have such a close and loving family.

Sunday December 24

> Everywhere...everywhere, Christmas tonight!
> Christmas in lands of the fir tree and pine,
> Christmas in lands of the palm tree and vine,
> Christmas where snowpeaks stand solemn and white
> Christmas where cornfields lie sunny and bright,
> Everywhere...everywhere, Christmas tonight!
>
> *Phillips Brooks*

Monday December 25

Christmas Day

THESE lines from Charles Dickens' *A Christmas Carol* seem to say it best.

"And it was always said of him that he knew how to keep Christmas well....May that be truly said of us, and all of us! And so, as Tiny Tim observed, God bless us, Every One!"

Tuesday December 26

BOXING Day gets its name from the English custom of giving Christmas boxes of food and money to family servants, tradespeople and others. The boxes were usually little earthenware boxes that were carried from house to house to collect tips and year-end bonuses. My grandson Marshall jokingly suggested that he carry one of these boxes door-to-door to collect enough to pay for the Christmas gifts that he purchased.

Wednesday December 27

Wintertime

The sound of distant sleigh-bells heard,
Sparkling snow upon the ground,
Wintertime! The very word
Has a pleasant cozy sound.

Youngsters on toboggan sleds,
Sliding down an icy hill,
Woolen caps upon their heads,
Laughter ringing, gay and shrill.

Merrily the back-logs blaze,
Roasting chestnuts, popping corn,
Do you recall the winter days
On the farm where you were born?

Winter in the city? No—
No one knows its dazzling charm
Unless they've seen untrodden snow
On the fields around a farm.

Isla Paschal Richardson

Thursday December 28

FOR God so loved the world, that he gave his only begotten Son, that whosoever believeth in him should not perish, but have everlasting life.

John 3:16

Friday December 29

The lovely phrase "remember when"
Sets every heart aglow,
As we drift back in memory
To the happy long ago.

Author unknown

Saturday December 30

MY friend Jake offered this amusing look at "senior citizens."

"A senior citizen is one who was here before the population explosion. We were here before television, penicillin, polio shots, antibiotics and Frisbees. We were here before frozen foods, nylon, Xerox and radar—before fluorescent lights, bank cards and ballpoint pens.

For us, time-sharing meant togetherness, not rental units. Hardware meant hardware and software wasn't even a word. We were before icemakers, dishwashers, clothes dryers, freezers, electric blankets or microwave ovens.

We were before men wore earrings and women wore tuxedos.

We got married and *then* lived together.

Bunnies were rabbits and rabbits were not Volkswagens.

We were before Batman, Barbie dolls, Cheerios, instant coffee or decaffeinated anything. There was no McDonald's and "fast food" was what you ate during Lent.

We were before the Beatles, Elvis, FM radio, tape recorders, word processors, call waiting and heavy metal music.

In our day, cigarette smoking was fashionable, grass was for mowing and coke was a refreshing drink.

We are today's senior citizens, a pretty hardy

bunch when you think how our world has changed and how we have had to adjust!"

Sunday December 31

ASK, and it shall be given you; seek, and ye shall find; knock, and it shall be opened unto you. For everyone that asketh receiveth; and he that seeketh findeth; and to him that knocketh it shall be opened.

Luke 11:9–10

As the year ends I hope that we may pause and reflect on all that we have to be grateful for.

Health, the love of friends and family, and happiness in the small joys of everyday living make this world a wonderful place to be.

May you look forward to a Happy New Year!